AF326709

LAUNCH <u>YOUR</u> RETIREMENT

Launch Your Retirement™

Your Financial Planning Guide for Going from Saver to Spender

© 2024 Ted Thatcher

ISBN (hardback): 978-1-964046-24-2
ISBN (paperback): 978-1-956220-56-8

www.ExpertPress.net

Expert Press
2 Shepard Hills Court
Little Rock, AR 72223
www.ExpertPress.net

Editing by Sandra Wendel
Proofreading by Geena Barret
Cover design by Be Authentic Productions

LAUNCH <u>YOUR</u> RETIREMENT

YOUR FINANCIAL PLANNING GUIDE FOR GOING FROM SAVER TO SPENDER

TED THATCHER

FINANCIAL ADVISOR

To my wife:

To my beloved wife, thank you for your endless support and love.

To my kids:

To my wonderful children, your curiosity inspires me every day.

To my clients:

To my esteemed clients, thank you for your trust and loyalty.

CONTENTS

PART ONE

INTRODUCTION

SPENDING MY YOUTH

ON A FARM

TAUGHT ME TO ALWAYS

DO YOUR BEST.

WHAT YOU PLANT NOW

YOU WILL HARVEST

LATER.

GROWING UP

"TEDDY, WHAT'S THE MEANING OF INTEGRITY?"

I always remember a dinner I attended as a child. My family and I and my uncle's family and a slew of cousins were going out to my grandfather's favorite place to eat. Papa was planning to retire that year, at sixty-six years of age, so he wanted to celebrate in his favorite restaurant.

Fourteen of us filed into the popular Italian restaurant and, as we were taking our seats, the server came up and asked what we would like to drink for refreshments for the evening. My grandmother let her know that tonight we were just going to be having water to drink. Then Grandma grabbed a menu, stood up, looked around the edges of the table and pointed to the menu and said, "Tonight, you can only order off this section right here."

That was a section with the chicken and the pasta—the lower-priced options on the menu. You must understand who my grandparents were. My grandfather was a grain farmer in a small town. He was the kind of guy that when you shook that man's hand, you thought you were going to lose yours. When we would gather at a dinner table like that, he would go around the table and quiz each of us grandkids.

He would say things like, "Teddy, what's the meaning of integrity?" I had heard that one before, so I piped up. "Integrity is what you do when no one's watching. It's having character, even if there's going to be a consequence."

My grandmother was the kindest person you have ever met in your whole life. She was loving and caring. She was always happy. She never failed to have something encouraging to say. She literally called us grandkids her sugar, spice, and everything nice. That was the kind of woman she was.

Yet despite the nature of her personality, which radiated joy, happiness, and love, she was worried as she sat there that day—worried that she and my grandfather were not going to have enough money in their retirement. They weren't really leaving the farm because their home is on our family compound. But my grandfather was stepping away from the day-to-day operation, leaving the work to my uncle, who also lived on the farm. This was a big transition for both of them.

She was anxious about not having enough money at a time when the only thing she should have been worried about was celebrating her husband of over forty years. Thus the plea to only order chicken.

I suspect you have asked yourself some of these questions:

- *When should I retire?*
- *If I retire and there is another financial crisis, am I going to have to go back to work?*

Whether that financial crisis is a high-inflation environment, a dot-com bubble burst, like we had in 2001, or a housing bubble burst, like we had in 2008, if you are retired or approaching retirement, you may be asking yourself these questions too:

- *Am I going to have to go back to work (or delay my retirement)?*
- *Am I going to be okay?*
- *Is my family going to be okay?*
- *Can we afford our mortgage?*

I believe your retirement, your "golden years" as they are so often referred to, should not be filled with that constant question about whether you are going to have enough money to pay your monthly bills or travel to see the national parks or pay for college for the grandkids. That's why every single day I sit down with families like yours, and we figure out the answer to those questions. We figure out what retirement is going to look like, how to distribute from investment accounts, and how to structure retirement income.

While we are answering that question, we spend a lot of time talking about legacy, because I recognize, as a financial planner, that what we leave behind as our legacy is an important part of the overall picture. It is as much about the imprint left behind as it is about who we are today. Legacy is a huge part of what we do in our personal lives. Because of that, I would like to share a bit of my own.

My great-grandfather, Myron William Thatcher, or M. W. Thatcher, was a successful and accomplished man. He helped start the grain cooperatives in the Midwest where my family comes from. Farmers back in the 1930s did not have the huge machinery and the ability to move large amounts of grain the way they do today.

Rural Americans lived on small family farms like ours, and they all had an issue: They had modest-sized crops, modest means of harvesting, and when they tried to sell their corn and soybeans, they had a hard time transporting the yield to market. No one had large transport trucks that we see today hauling grain. That meant when they did go to sell their excess crop, they had a hard time getting a fair price for it.

My great-grandfather recognized this dilemma and said, "What we're going to do is come together and create a collective—a co-op. All the farmers are going to have part ownership. And we're going to create a series of grain elevators along the railroad so our farmers can then bring and store their grain together in large quantities along a supply chain. That way we can collectively bargain and get a fair price for our grain."

Grain elevators were built in small towns throughout the Midwest, and the co-ops allowed farmers to be more profitable. It was an overwhelming success. You can still see these large grain storage bins and the elevators in whistle-stop towns, close to the rail lines, that transport the farmers' grain from trucks into the sky-high circular structures for storage.

Three presidents wanted my great-grandfather in their administrations. John F. Kennedy wanted him to be head of the Department of Agriculture. They wanted him because of his accomplishments, but they also wanted him because they wanted farmers' votes. He turned them down. He simply wanted to help make the lives of other farmers better and ensure that his interests were aligned with theirs.

With that kind of background, you might not be surprised to learn that many of my family members are farmers. We have a

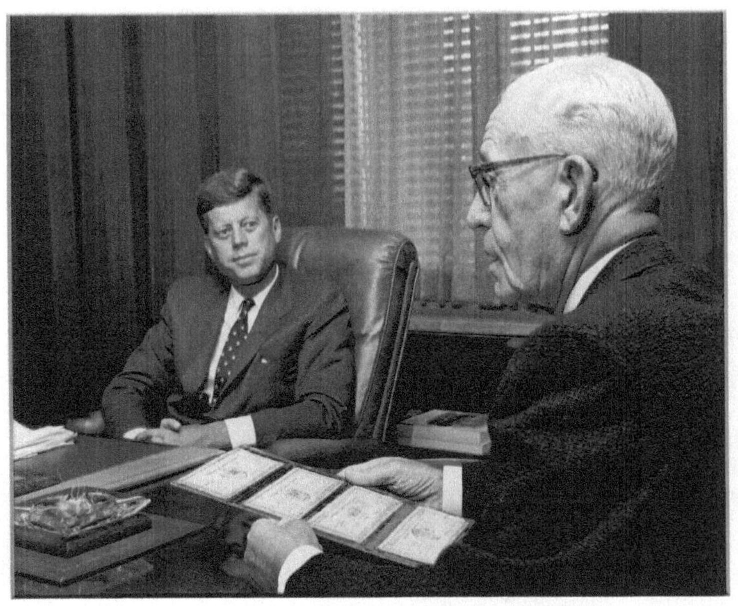

John F. Kennedy ~ M.W. Thatcher
Presidential Campaign ~ 1961

fifth-generation family farm now that has grown quite large—into the thousands and thousands of acres, still in southern Michigan. We have an armada of huge machinery.

When we were kids, we basically grew up in and around the farmhouse. My grandmother and grandfather, Nana and Papa, had a house adjacent to the farm. My great-uncle Ted and his wife, just like my grandfather, lived in a home on an L-shaped lot adjacent to my grandparents' farmhouse on the corner of the farm.

Altogether, counting my brothers, cousins, and me, there were sixteen grandchildren on that family farm—a gaggle of young kids. The world we lived in when we were growing up was the farm world. We grew up at a time when our parents just said, "Hey, we'll see you at dinnertime." And that was my childhood: Go play with your cousins on the farm, and we'll see you later. We would go and just adventure together. Often it felt as if we had our own sports team running around out there. We would have field days as a family on the huge lawn behind the two main houses. And we would play volleyball and football and anything under the sun.

I have a large framed photo of the family farm in my office to remind me of my legacy. I often gaze at the huge barns and the towering grain elevators—and to think we would climb on top of them. We would drive machinery around long before anybody was old enough to have a driver's license. We would fly around on four wheelers and golf carts chasing each other. My cousins, brothers, and I would climb on the tractors, and during harvest, we'd be diving into these grain containers, swimming in humongous containers of corn and soybeans. Looking back, it was an amazing way to grow up.

When I was young, I had my cousins to be with, and that was plenty. With anybody outside of that group, I was always a bit shy. As I grew older, I became a much more outgoing person.

Dinner at my grandma's house was always a huge meal with a roast in the oven, mashed potatoes and gravy, and toast. And it didn't have to be Thanksgiving to have cranberry sauce. My grandfather insisted on having it with his meals. My Nana had an expansive sunroom just next to the kitchen where amazing smells would emerge. Nobody would be on a cell phone at the table. We would listen to the adults, and we would occasionally be asked to speak.

I learned a lot just listening to the stories that my uncles and aunts and grandparents would tell. They were great storytellers with big personalities, and they would have a lot of fun doing it. We didn't realize it at the time, but we kids were learning life lessons at the dinner table.

TAKING ACTION

WHAT I LEARNED AND HOW LIFE LESSONS
LED ME TO FINANCIAL PLANNING

What did all of this teach me? I recognized that I wanted to do meaningful things with meaningful people: people who mean a lot to me, people I love. My goal became having meaningful work and meaningful relationships.

I began to put that goal into action when I was eighteen. My best friends from high school and I formed a nonprofit called Acts of Random Kindness, or ARK. The idea behind our little organization was a "pay it forward" model where we would do an act of random kindness. Some of them were big, some of them were small. The only thing we would ask is that in some form or fashion the individual who received that act of kindness would simply pay it forward. The goal, and the mission, was to inspire what we called an epidemic of kindness.

Some of my buddies and I convinced a nice couple to sell us their ancient RV for a few thousand dollars. Once we purchased it, we gutted the interior and put four bunk beds in the back. I, along with my best buddy, Alex, my brother Jacob, another of our close friends, Dalton, and a guy named Jesse all joined in.

We put together a list of kind acts that we wanted to do. We acquired some cameras and then we took off on a 10,000-mile road trip around the country, checking off the list as we went. Some of the acts were simple, such as helping folks change a tire on the side of the road. Others were more complex, such as taking the kids from the Boys and Girls Club in San Francisco to a Giants game or Disneyland. We would take families in need on shopping trips or hand out ice water on the street in steamy hot Las Vegas.

Our venture succeeded beyond our imaginations. We were able to impact thousands of people across the country that year. We even ended up on *The Today Show* and had the opportunity to share our story. We partnered with some big brands, such as Yum, which owns franchises like Pizza Hut and Taco Bell. We received grants from the Ford Motor Company. KIND snacks became a partner, along with Thor Motor Coach and Lippert Components. They helped sponsor a second tour.

I started college at Miami University in Ohio and transitioned to another educational setting on the West Coast. I knew I wanted to be in business, so ultimately connections led me to the next chapter of my life.

I joined a private equity company that focused on commodities as an investment analyst. It was a lucrative career path, but before long, I discovered I did not like working in a cubicle.

Growing up, I had loved math. I am definitely a numbers guy. I love investments, but I did not enjoy working in a private equity firm. As I was sifting through my options, I remembered that restaurant dinner with my grandparents, when my grandmother was worried on what should have been a day of celebration.

Despite a lifetime of hard work, my grandparents did not know if they had enough money saved to take care of themselves in retirement. I realized financial planning and advising was a way to achieve my life's mission: to do meaningful work with meaningful people, just as we had done on our RV road trip. I knew that I would be able to provide a tremendous amount of value to my clients from an investment standpoint, but I also wanted to make sure to pair that with the legacy piece: the purpose behind retirement.

> **I wanted to create a company that would reflect my values, what life and legacy is truly about.**

My approach to financial planning was not envisioned to be a flash-in-the-pan approach. It would be something that would mature and be there for a long time.

NEXT STEPS

CORE VALUES THAT DRIVE MY PASSION
FOR FINANCIAL PLANNING

With these goals in mind, I created my company. At Bright Lake, my team and I have adopted three core values that have served us and our clients well: sincere candor, unimpeachable character, and competitive greatness. I'll touch on each briefly.

SINCERE CANDOR

When I meet with people I advise, I always ask myself two questions: "Do I believe that I can make a significant impact in your financial life?" and "Do I believe this is a good fit?" That second question may surprise you, but I ask it because next month, a year from now, five years from now, or twenty years from now, when we schedule a visit with our clients, when I see that meeting on my calendar, I want to look forward to it. I want to set up all our clients for future success.

My team at Bright Lake strives to have a clear and open relationship with each of our clients. We need them to be fully open with us. We are going to be fully open with them, with investment strategies we think they could benefit from as well as what we believe they should invest their money and passion in. We provide a candid perspective on where they are in their wealth-building journey. Are they prepared for retirement or are there issues they need to address? They need the clear-cut, straightforward truth.

If our clients are on the edge of being able to retire or not, they need to know that. They also need to know what they might change to get to that point, if that is their situation. They may very well have a lot of financial strategies they could improve on to maximize their retirement.

A lot of the folks that we work with really care about stewardship. When I can see someone is able to retire but they haven't set up a plan to optimize it yet, I've often found myself using the phrase good to great: "John and Mary, your situation is about going from good to great." This situation, this experience, is brand new to them. They have not made this transition to retirement before.

When people have built up a sizable net worth, I will say, "You are the CEO of a seven-figure enterprise now. You must make some serious decisions, because a 10 percent wrong decision now is a whole lot of money. It is $100,000. Or it could be a 10 percent pay cut when it comes to your retirement income." If we are off just a little bit, now that we have this serious net worth, it can mean a huge cost. To use a scuba diving expression, a diver would say, "If you miss by an inch, you miss by a mile."

When you are walking through this phase of planning out a retirement, it is important to make sure you have the right sort of CFO—a chief financial officer, so to speak—come alongside you and help manage the biggest transition of your financial life. Or, to put it another way, it is important to make sure you have the right copilot helping you land the plane as you navigate retirement.

UNIMPEACHABLE CHARACTER

This trait comes down to how my company and I operate from an ethics perspective. When it comes to the management of your investments, we operate with a fiduciary standard of care, which means we must put the client's best interest above our own. When we sit down with a client, we want them to know what is going to be in their best interest, even if it's not the most fun news to hear. It is extremely important to us to do everything we can to put our clients in the best position to win.

You may think, "Well, don't all financial service professionals have this obligation?" and certainly, that would make sense. Perhaps surprisingly, it certainly is not the case.

Which is why we take our role as financial guides with extreme humbleness and honor. And as my grandfather had asked me many times at the dinner table, "Teddy, what's the meaning of integrity?" my answer, "Integrity is what you do when no one's watching. It's having character, even if there's going to be a consequence," became a foundation for my company decades later.

COMPETITIVE GREATNESS

This is so important to me because it reflects upon our mission. We want folks to be able to live a retirement worth sharing. My team and I are not here just to manage money. We are not here just making sure you have as many dollars as possible at the end of your life. We are here to help you realize the retirement you have always dreamed of.

When I talk with clients, I observe what they smile about, what brings them joy, and therein lies the answer to what they invest their time into. It is about what kinds of relationships they have with those closest to them.

Think back to my brief example of John and Mary. They went through their life together, they raised a family, they became empty nesters, they finished their careers. Now they have all this time back, and a great opportunity to have a totally new relationship with one another and with their friends and other family members.

What kinds of relationships do they want with their kids and grandkids? How do they want that to change? Maybe they want to invest more time giving back by volunteering at their church or another organization in their community. Maybe they want to coach a sports team. I really encourage folks to think not just about the fact that they want to retire, but to really think about what they want to retire to.

We help our clients realize an excellent, fulfilling retirement worth sharing. When they enter our office, we want them to know beyond a shadow of a doubt that we are not like other firms. We aren't here to throw a bunch of stock market data, spreadsheets, and mumbo jumbo at people and walk them out the door.

Our goal is your goal: We are here to help guide you to live a retirement as unique as your fingerprint.

When folks come into our office, they are not sitting in a crowded lobby as if they are waiting to see their dentist. We give them privacy. They are immediately walked into one of our conference rooms—one named after my grandfather, the other after my great-uncle—so they have their own private and confidential space. They are immediately offered drinks and snacks from a menu of options while they wait for one of our launch advisors to come in. We have homemade cookies, toasted and warmed and brought to them along with a little tray of nuts.

We do this because we believe if something is worth doing, it is worth doing right. We believe the small things matter as much as the big things and that how you do one thing is how you do every-thing—whether that is something as simple as the way we say hello or as important as providing investment analysis. From the moment an individual enters our environment, we want them to know that we are here to provide them exceptional service. A white-glove experience.

It is difficult to overstate the importance of sound and smart fi-nancial planning, and my grandparents' story is just one example of why. I would say the two most significant points of change in your financial life are when you get married and when you make the transi-tion to retirement. By a wide margin, from a technical standpoint, the transition to retirement is much more complex.

I started our firm so that others would not have to face the ques-tion my grandparents did. So that our clients could realize the retire-ment they had always dreamed of. I believe everyone should have that opportunity and that everyone should be able to answer the question, "How do I retire more confidently?"

I have written this book to share with you the step-by-step process I believe is necessary to Launch Your Retirement™.

Let's get started.

PART 2

THE FIVE PILLARS

WHEN YOU BUILD A

HOUSE, YOU'RE NOT

SIMPLY CREATING A

STRUCTURE; YOU'RE

SHAPING THE

FUTURE BY TAKING

CONTROL OF EVERY

DETAIL.

WHAT ARE THE FIVE PILLARS

BUILD YOUR FINANCIAL HOUSE

Donna came into our office a few years ago. We prepared her for her eventual retirement from the insurance company where she had worked for thirty years. During our planning sessions, she had talked about wanting to take her granddaughters to Disneyland.

So once she retired, she withdrew a lump sum from her retirement accounts, which we had structured so that distributing it minimized the tax consequences, and off they went to Anaheim.

When she returned, I tell you what: I have never seen someone have a bigger smile on her face than Donna did when she was telling us about that trip to Disneyland. It is the happiest place on earth, and Donna found true joy there.

At the Bibbidi Bobbidi Boutique—a reference, of course, to Cinderella and the fairy godmother, inside the big blue castle at Disneyland—she took her granddaughters there to be transformed into their favorite Disney princess for the day. Some girls choose Cinderella. Some choose Belle from Beauty and the Beast. More recently, they may choose Elsa from Frozen or Rapunzel from Tangled.

Donna told us about how her granddaughters, ages eight and ten, had their hair done and put on a princess dress and donned a tiara and wand and glitter and make-up. It was the most incredible experience for them. As she was sharing this memory and the many iPhone photos, her face just glowed, she was so happy. Honestly, this is an emotional memory for me, because it is moments like this that make all the planning, all the work, worthwhile.

Together, we prepare our clients like Donna for the life they are retiring to. People often think of retirement as a departure, as something they are leaving. But it is simply a gateway to the next stage of life. We do the planning specifically so that our clients can comfortably and confidently step into that special new season of life. That is what building your financial house is about.

THE FIVE PILLARS:

- **Income planning**
- **Investment planning**
- **Tax planning**
- **Healthcare planning**
- **Legacy planning**

Over the next five chapters, I will introduce you to the five pillars of a holistic financial plan for your retirement. They are the building blocks of your Disneyland experience. No magic. Just smart planning. And I will explain how we bring them all together and build your financial house properly so that you can maximize your retirement.

By building your financial house using these five pillars, you can move into retirement confidently. To use a scriptural analogy, you can think of it as having your house built on solid rock rather than on shifting sand. For many of us, there are so many things that cause uncertainty about retirement, and without the proper structure, it is easy to feel you are sinking into the shifting sands.

Our holistic Launch Your Retirement™ Blueprint planning process (see graphic on following page) incorporates all these pillars in a synergistic approach where they work in tandem to create your fiscal house. Have you ever built a house or had one built for you? Would you even consider doing that without a blueprint? You would not build a house by starting with a living room and then jump over to a bedroom and then add a bathroom. You follow a blueprint until the entire house comes together.

We do the same thing when we build a retirement plan. We do not just MacGyver it along the way. We cannot neglect any part of that plan as we go along. If we do not do the electrical or we don't have insulation in the walls, or we don't have the proper framing, it is not going to be a solid, well-functioning house. Maybe it won't collapse right away, but it's a long way from optimized. When we have built your financial house, that means you have a complete financial plan.

LAUNCH YOUR RETIREMENT™
BLUEPRINT

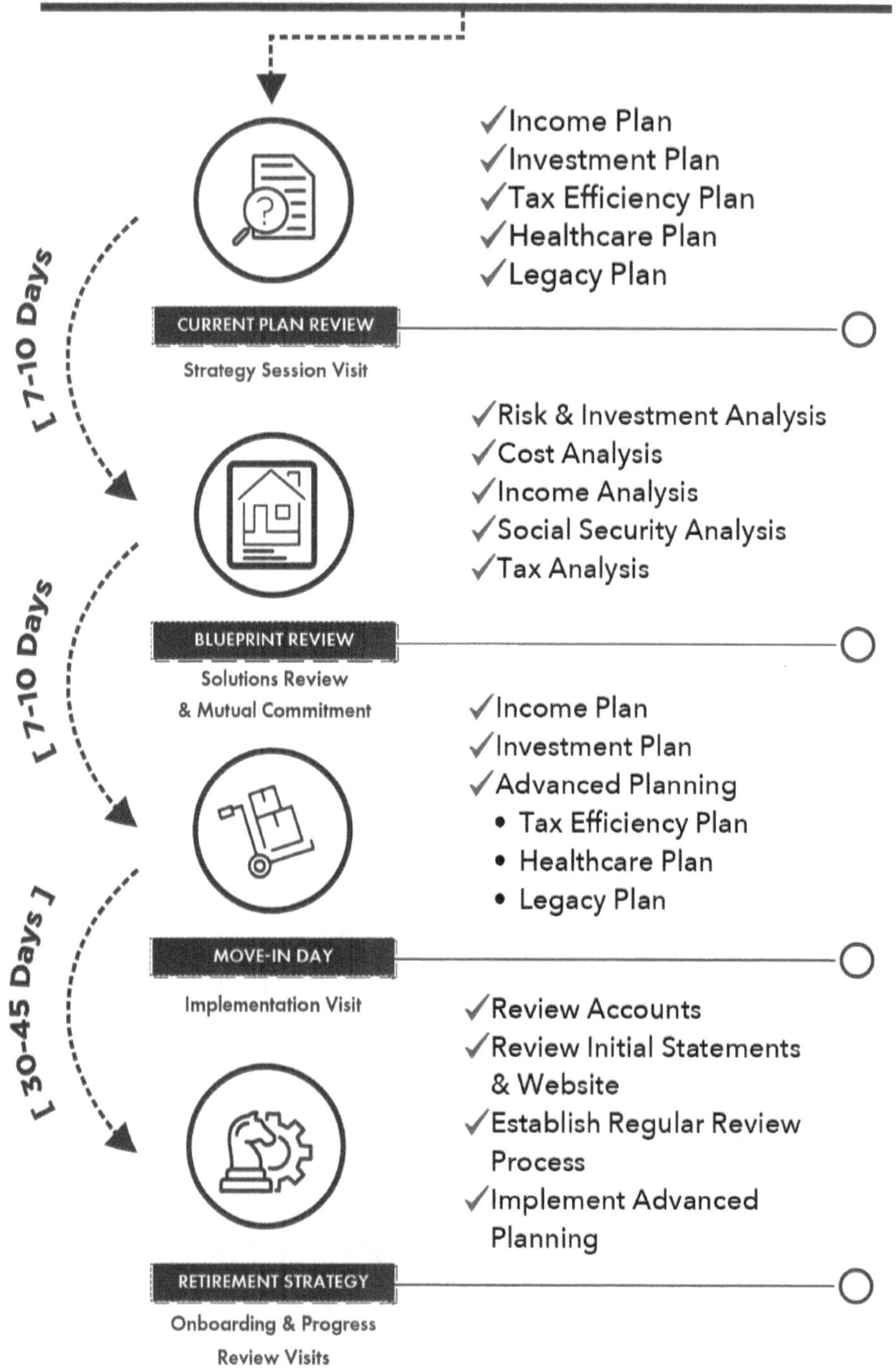

Once your financial house is built, your golden goose (this is your nest egg, your financial wealth) gets to live in it like the turkey pardoned by the president every Thanksgiving. That turkey knows going forward that he is taken care of. He is confident and at ease, knowing he is safe and secure.

Building a house is quite an endeavor—from little pieces such as nails, screws, and glue to large items such as beams and concrete slabs. They all work together to create your house. There can be many pieces to your financial house as well: stocks, bonds, mutual funds, and various types of investments, annuities, and insurance. We pull them all together and organize them in a way that maximizes your retirement.

When Henry Ford rolled out the Model T, people used to joke, "You can choose any color you want—as long as it's black." So many residential developments these days like to say, "Build your dream home!"—provided it is one of two or three floor plans they offer.

Your financial house should not be anything like that. **Your retirement plan should be as unique as your fingerprint, tailored to your needs.** Think of your financial house as a structure to organize your assets in a way that provides the retirement you want. When you lay your head down on your pillow at night, instead of wondering how all your various accounts that you have accumulated over the years—that old 401(k) or a 403(b) that you had at another job, or an IRA—are going to be part of your retirement, you should be able to go to sleep knowing that you have taken the appropriate steps to organize your financial life and set yourself up for long-term success.

If you are going to build that house, what do you need to do? What are the practical steps? First, you need to select your architect. This is going to be a financial advisor. But they should be more than that—they should be a guide too. They should guide you through this process so you understand it as you go. It is not enough to choose an advisor and then tell them, "You take care of it," dust off your hands, and walk out the door. **You need to be involved and have a voice in what your financial house looks like.**

As I write this, I think to myself how great a privilege it is to be that architect for our clients. Whoever you use to help you build your financial house, I believe a few things should be true of that person. First, I believe that they should have to operate with a fiduciary standard of care. This means they have a legal obligation to always operate in your best interest when managing your investments.

Did you know only a small percentage of financial services professionals have a fiduciary obligation to their clients. I'll explain what fiduciary means in more depth in the next chapter, but briefly, it means the financial advisor has a legal obligation—a duty—to act in your best interest.

Along with being a fiduciary, second, I believe they should be **independent**. They should not be just showing you one or two companies' financial funds. This often happens at many firms where there are financial incentives to do so.

My third recommendation is that they be **experienced**. They need to concentrate in the type of planning that you need (in other words, there's a big difference between an accumulation advisor and a retirement advisor). They should have walked through retirement with folks many times and have planned many retirements. They should be well versed in helping people establish these different pillars in their financial houses.

To repeat the qualities I recommend you look for in a financial advisor, they should have to operate with a fiduciary standard of care, they should be independent, and they should be experienced.

These are the guidelines I recommend using when selecting your financial advisor, the architect and guide, for helping build your financial house and your plan as a whole. When you make your choice and sit down with them, make sure that person has the appropriate understanding of your situation, what your current investment plan looks like, what your current income plan is, and what your tax plan looks like. If those parameters are not established, it is like trying to build a house without all the materials you need.

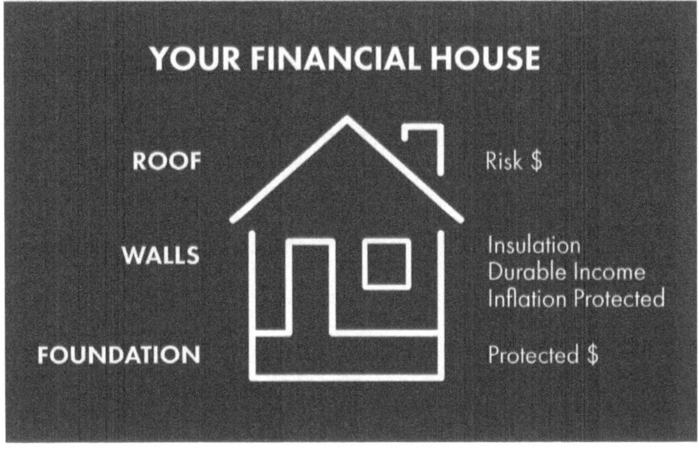

You will be making all kinds of choices from the many options you have available. How much in stocks, bonds, and mutual funds do you want to have? What insurance do you need for healthcare planning? What insurance, if any, do you need for long-term care? What documents do you need in place for legacy planning? Think of all those pieces as construction materials.

> **Once you have your blueprint , the construction begins, and the plans that have been outlined get implemented.**

Think of this process as building a house unique to you: Are you going to have your dream kitchen, a chef's kitchen, in your custom home? Are you going to do a double oven? Will there be quartz or granite countertops? What kinds of finishes do you want? Are you going to put a swimming pool in your backyard? Or perhaps a firepit? Will you have an in-home cinema with surround sound and theater seating? Will you install a temperature-controlled wine cellar in the basement or design a spacious tool shed in the back of the property so you can tinker with various hobbies?

When you have the architect appointed, the blueprints done, and the materials selected, then it is just a matter of pulling the trigger and implementing it. Compare the process to moving into your dream home. You have taken the proper steps, you have found the guide who is right for you, you have done the necessary work, and now you get to live it out. Once your house is built on that solid rock, you get to move on to what retirement is truly about: making the most of this stage of your life. And you may not be dreaming of princesses at Disneyland, like Donna, but you certainly have dreams. It is time to realize them.

THE FIVE PILLARS SUMMARY:

1. Retirement as a New Chapter: Retirement is a new beginning, good planning allows you to achieve your dreams.

2. Constructing Your Financial House: Create a "financial house" tailored to your needs, providing stability and peace of mind.

3. Five Pillars of Financial Planning: Learn the five essential pillars that form a solid foundation for a secure retirement.

4. Choosing the Right Financial Advisor: Select an advisor who is a fiduciary, independent, and experienced.

5. Active Participation Is Key: Stay involved in the planning process and ensure your plan meets your needs.

ACTION STEPS:

- **Review Your Plan: Ensure it aligns with your retirement goals.**

- **Select the Right Advisor: Choose a qualified advisor.**

- **Be Proactive: Regularly update and adjust your plan.**

PILLAR 1

"THOSE WHO FAIL TO PLAN,
PLAN TO FAIL."

— *BENJAMIN FRANKLIN* —

INCOME PLANNING

HOW TO MAKE THE MOST OF THE
TRANSITION FROM SAVER TO SPENDER

Income planning is the first pillar in building your sturdy financial house. The importance of retirement planning overall cannot be overstated. Broken down into its most basic elements, your financial life is divided into two phases: saving assets during your working years and then spending assets during your retirement years.

When you transition from saver to spender, you need a retirement plan. We call our planning process the Launch Your Retirement™ Blueprint, and each blueprint is distinct to the family or individual we are drafting it for. Your retirement is as unique as you are; therefore, your retirement plan should not be a cookie cutter, like a tract home; it should be as unique to you as your fingerprint. Each blueprint is built on the five pillars I introduced earlier. Income planning is the first pillar I will explain in more depth so you can see your financial house will be based on a sturdy foundation. Let's take a closer look at income planning.

The first of the five aspects of income planning is an income and expense analysis. At Bright Lake, we start with the end in mind and reverse engineer from there. This is the framework of income planning. We start by defining your goal. What are you shooting for?

> **ASSETS: Valuable things you own, like a house, car, or savings, that can help you financially in the future.**

Remember the childhood story of the goose that laid the golden eggs? I refer to that goose when discussing retirement planning with my clients: "Frank and Barbara, you have built up this nest egg. You have this golden goose in front of you. We want to make sure that goose lives a long time. We don't want to kill the goose. We want the goose to lay those golden eggs for you throughout retirement. We don't want your assets to shrink away."

There are many threats to your golden goose: Inflation. Taxes. (I will sometimes say Uncle Sam is out there hunting your goose with a shotgun.) We have volatility in the financial markets. All kinds of different expenses can come up for retirees, such as family emergencies or significant medical events.

REPLACING YOUR PAYCHECK WITH A PLAY CHECK

When I talk about "replacing" your paycheck, I first make sure your baseline expenses are covered. There are a lot of ways we can do that. We will start by going through a budget worksheet. We want to know what your expenses look like today.

Baseline expenses would be what you expect to pay each month for such items as mortgage, groceries, utilities, transportation, and insurance.

Frequently, someone who is not retired yet will say, "I don't know what my retirement budget is going to look like." I push back by saying, "You know what? You would be surprised how accurate we can be with what your budget might look like in retirement, even if we just have a good idea of what your expenses look like today."

Along with replacing your paycheck, we also want to make sure you have a "play check" so you can do the activities you have always wanted to do. This will allow you to live the retirement that you have always dreamed of in the way that you have dreamed it.

Establishing our two "checks"—the paycheck and the play check—gives us something to shoot for. We can then systematically reverse engineer the plan from there. But your plan should be about more than just how much your spending each month. It should include what you're planning on retiring to. And that's unique to you.

Where do you want to invest your time? Maybe it is coaching a sports team, like Little League baseball or a youth basketball team. Maybe it is an array of community service or community involvement.

A part-time retirement job. Travel. Getting serious about a hobby. Wintering in Arizona. Perhaps it is wanting to spend time with your friends or your spouse or grandchildren in a new and special way.

Making a transition to retirement gives you an opportunity to have an entirely different relationship with your spouse. You very likely had a career, raised a family, became an empty nester, and finished your career. Now you have your spouse sitting there and a fresh opportunity to have a new relationship with them. Or you are single or a widow or widower. Asking "What's next?" might look different for you now. Explore how you would like to make the most of your situation.

In fact, let's define what your perfect day looks like. Where are you? What are you doing? Who are you with? How do you feel? Maybe it is on a beach, maybe you're hiking in a national park or on the road in an RV, or maybe you are on a Disney adventure with your kids or grandkids, or you're taking everybody out to dinner and you're celebrating someone. How many of those perfect days did you have last year? Maybe it was ten or seven or three. But let's make sure that next year you have more of those perfect days. And the year after that you have still more of those perfect days.

Knowing what your perfect day looks like is a big part of the income and expense analysis. As part of developing a retirement blueprint, we will do a stress test on your money to calculate how long your money can last, because that is the number one question that folks are asking.

A Gallup poll in 2018 revealed 54 percent of Americans ask one question more than any other when it comes to their retirement: **"Am I going to outlive my money?"** They may express that concern in a variety of ways: "Am I going to be able to do what I want to do?" "Will I be able to take the trips I want to take?" "Is there enough money to pay for my grandkids' college education?" "Will medical bills wipe out our savings?" I think everyone is asking those kinds of questions.

IRA:	ROTH IRA:	401(k):
Tax advantaged account for saving for retirement.	Retirement account where money grows tax free.	A retirement plan offered by your employer with tax benefits.

When we do the income and expense analysis and the stress test, we'll learn how much income your portfolio can produce and discover whether you'll have a lot of money or if you're flying too close to the sun and need to make changes.

One aspect of planning that too many people—and, too often, advisors—ignore is where the distributions from their investment accounts will be coming from. The answer to that question will have tax implications. Are they just coming from an IRA? Is it from a trust or a brokerage account or a Roth IRA?

Advisors often talk about asset allocation. But I don't hear nearly enough advisors talking about asset location. When I say asset location, I am talking about what tax buckets these moneys are in. Many Americans save just in their qualified account, and that might be a traditional 401(k) or a traditional IRA. That is all taxable, so when we think about how long your money can last, we need to think about how we're going to structure these distributions in a tax-efficient way.

RETIREMENT RISK ZONE

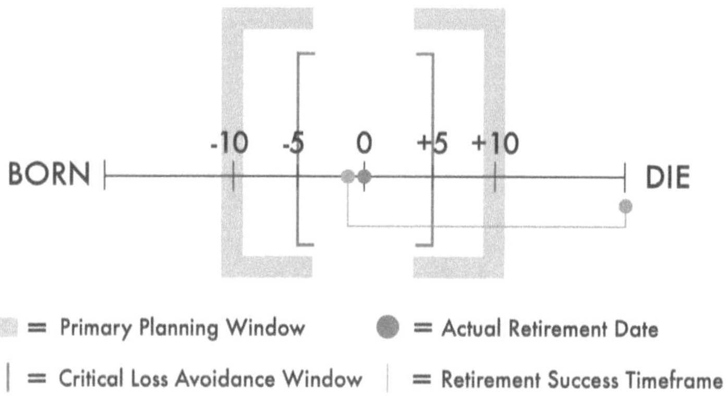

My client Dale worked for a company for twenty-five years. He was sixty-five when we discussed his retirement plan. He was about to go on Medicare. Dale and his wife, Michelle, had been on his health insurance for his entire working career. She was sixty-two, so when he goes on Medicare, she will no longer be on his employer's plan and will have to shop for health insurance on the open market.

If they are not careful—and I see this all the time—people will take too much in distributions out of a taxable source, so they will not be eligible for a health insurance subsidy through the Affordable Care Act, commonly known as Obamacare. Your income must be lower than certain limits set by the government related to poverty levels to take advantage of the health insurance marketplace subsidies for health insurance. As a result, a lot of people, like Michelle, cannot retire before they turn sixty-five. Finding affordable health insurance is what keeps many people working up until they're eligibile for Medicare (age sixty-five).

MAKING THE Social Security DECISION

Another key element in your income planning is maximizing your Social Security. I often call this the million-dollar decision. I hear advisors all the time simply say, "Just file for Social Security when you retire. Everything will be fine." But that is not good enough, in my opinion. Or that simple.

Unless you run the numbers for you and your family's situation, you are not going to know how to maximize your benefits. People put hardly any analysis into it at all. They just go by their gut or ask what their golfing buddy does. I teach classes on understanding your Social Security benefits. I typically start the classes by helping set expectations for those in the class.

I explain what is called the 60/40 premise. If you are an average American who earns an average American family's wage, about 60 percent of your retirement income would be coming from sources

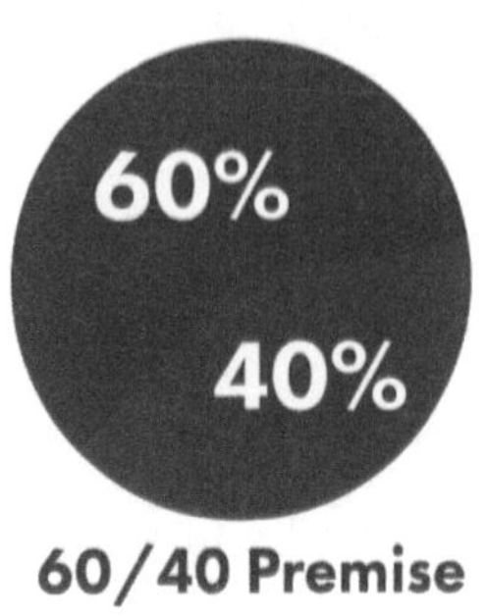

60/40 Premise

outside of Social Security—say, a pension, a 401(k), perhaps rental property or other investments. In turn, that would mean the average American would expect their Social Security benefits at full retirement to cover about 40 percent of their retirement needs, according to the Social Security Administration.

These numbers are relative, however. Meaning if you are in a higher income tax bracket, Social Security is going to cover a lower amount of your monthly expenses. And certainly, if you are in a lower income tax bracket, Social Security is going to cover a higher amount of your monthly expenses.

What this all means is that, on average, your decision on when to start taking Social Security is going to affect 40 percent of your retirement income. Accordingly, you might want to put a considerable amount of thought into exactly how you are going to file. Unfortunately, I just don't see that happening. Generally, I tell my clients, "Don't just file when you retire without running the numbers first."

Beyond that 60/40 premise, Social Security is a monster that is extremely complicated. **Did you know that, for a married couple, there are more than 560 different ways you could collect your Social Security benefits?** Most people tell me they are considering just a handful of those options. They will say, "You know, Ted, I plan to file at sixty-two, as early as I can." Others will plan to file at age sixty-five, their Medicare age for full benefits. Still, others will say they want to wait until they turn seventy to try to get as large an amount of money as possible every month.

When to file for monthly Social Security checks is a critical decision.

Keep in mind that if you are asking those questions and considering those options, you are doing something awesome. You are trying to figure out how to get the most benefit—for you. But if you are only considering a few options or only know about a few options, you are probably missing out on some strategies that could be putting you into a significantly better financial situation.

When trying to figure out when and how to start receiving those monthly Social Security benefits, many people do this: They go to the Social Security office in their city and say, "I am trying to figure out how to maximize my benefits for my family's situation. Can you help me figure out exactly what to do?"

> **There is a significant difference between sound financial advice and simple information.**

Frankly, avoid this step.

The federal employees in your Social Security office are not able to provide financial advice. They do not have the financial licenses to be able to do that. I see folks butt heads with people at the Social Security office all the time because they ask a question looking for advice and what they get in return is just information. There is a significant difference between sound financial advice and simple information.

When we are talking about Social Security, we are in reality talking about retirement income planning, so you do need to get sound advice on it. For most people, information is not going to be enough. You should expect the same level of care, consideration, and analysis to be put into how you are going to be filing for Social Security as you would expect to be put into the management of your investments, your tax strategy, the distributions from your investment accounts, your estate plan, and anything else that is part of your retirement blueprint.

This is what our team does every day in our office. We sit down with folks and learn about their unique situations. We run the numbers on this with a lot of families. Filing in an incorrect way or an inefficient way may cost you well over $100,000. For a lot of families—I would even say a majority—this is a million-dollar decision we are making. And if we are 10 percent wrong, it is going to cost you more than $100,000.

WHAT IS YOUR INFLATION PLAN?

Another critical aspect of income planning is an inflation plan. Obviously, it is easy to talk about inflation because you can see it, at the grocery store and gas pump, in furniture prices and prices of just about everything.

> **The bottom line is this: Inflation must be one of the parts of income planning that we account for.**

But it is funny, because a few years ago that wasn't the case. Even in 2019, when I was telling folks about wanting to make sure we plan for inflation, I would have to stress this, "When we think about inflation, it is the straw that gets added and added and added over time. Eventually, it breaks the camel's back. It is a slow death."

The definition of inflation really has to do with buying power. It is how much you can truly buy with the money that you have. When we think about buying power, and how it gets eroded, I like to use this example: Even if we just use a modest inflation figure, say 2.5 percent a year, that inflationary percentage still packs a punch. If you have $10,000 of expenses today, twenty years from now it is going to be $20,000 worth of expenses, so even if 2.5 percent a year does not sound like much, it really adds up.

Another way to look at inflation is that trip you want to take with your family for $10,000 this year, in twenty years will cost you $20,000. When I brought up inflation a few years ago to our clients, they practically ignored me. Think about how prices have changed over time, such as the price of a loaf of bread or a gallon of milk, or even a gallon of gas back in the 1970s. These things were pennies on the dollar. The bottom line is this: Inflation must be one of the parts of income planning that we account for.

HAVE YOU ACCOUNTED FOR SPOUSAL INCOME?

Another aspect of income planning should consider spousal income, if that is applicable in your situation. Sometimes this is called survivorship income planning. What it boils down to is we want to make sure that, whichever spouse passes away first, the other spouse is going to be okay financially. If you have pensions, it is vital to think about the survivorship selections that you make on those pensions.

It is important to view Social Security through the lens of survivorship, so when a spouse passes away, you keep the higher of the two Social Security amounts and lose the other one. Particularly if there is a significant age gap, it's worth reviewing how your investments are going to be contributing to that.

This is important because 99 percent of people who are married do not die at the same time. If I am teaching at an event, I will pause and state, "For all the ladies in the room, it's time to focus, because this is one of the hardest and most difficult things to talk about when it comes to planning. It just is." Men die first. They just do.

I was talking with a couple not long ago. She said it is common for her and her husband to joke about who will die first because he is older. They have a federal pension. He only gets a 50 percent survivorship election on it. She will receive half if he dies before she does.

She likes to say to him, "Hey, honey, you can't die because I need that money."

I asked her, "I know you're joking about it, but do you actually have a written plan for what's going to happen to your income and how you're going to account for that drop in income?"

She said, "No."

Joking aside, this is a serious topic I cover with my clients. I know it is extremely difficult to talk about, but often that is when you're going to need an advisor to talk through some of those particularly difficult conversations so that you're not walking down a path with your eyes closed. **When it comes to income planning, you need to understand the options and not put your head in the sand.**

What this means is most of the time, married men will pass away married. Married women will pass away widowed. In either case, the surviving spouse is going to need that plan mapped out for how they are going to manage the entire financial situation in the event their spouse dies first. Well-meaning husbands are trying to provide for their families and build up savings so they can retire and their family can be financially stable. But what's amazing is that at the end of their life, it is actually their wife who often has to have her hands on the wheel.

My point is that, whatever your living arrangement, make sure everyone understands income planning and plans for all the scenarios regarding who dies first. **Work with a trusted advisor who shares your core values and whom you trust to help guide your spouse through those decisions.**

Social Security was never intended to be your sole source of income in retirement. Let's take a historical perspective. When Social Security was established during the Great Depression, the average life expectancy was fifty-eight for men and sixty-two for women. Since Social Security benefits were not paid until someone turned sixty-five, that meant many Americans received no payments at all. They never lived that long.

Thanks to the expansion of the middle class after World War II—meaning many more people could set money aside and not work until they died, along with significant improvements in medicine—it's not unusual for someone retiring today to live another twenty-five to thirty years after retirement.

Even if your relatives did not commonly live to reach 100, retirement accounts have to last longer now than they ever have. As a result, inflation needs to be a significant consideration when mapping out your income plan and survivorship plan.

How do we make sure to maintain your preferred standard of living over a longer period in the face of unrelenting inflation? We want to make sure that we are thinking about the structure of your

income distributions. We also must keep in mind that expenses may well rise when one spouse passes away. You now become a single filer when it comes to your taxes, which means that you are going to pay a higher tax rate on the exact same income than you were before as a married couple.

Beyond that, let's say the husband dies and he's the one who did all the household maintenance. The wife might not be able to do all those tasks herself, certainly in her older age, and so those jobs are likely going to all need to be hired out if they aren't already. That is another increased expense.

You may not even have the same income, depending on whether your late spouse had a pension and how any survivor benefit was set up. If you were both on Social Security, the lower of the two payouts goes away. People like to think, "When my spouse passes away, I'll live on less." And it is true you may not spend as much on food and miscellaneous expenses. But as I pointed out earlier, other expenses may well increase. And groceries, utilities, phone, and insurance may not be lower and will certainly rise with inflation.

In my experience, maybe only half of the time is a client's pension set up to be fully transferred to the surviving spouse. Pension recipients usually have that option, however, so if they plan ahead, we can make sure that they make the right selections on their pensions. But sometimes we learn that decision was already made and the transferable amount is only 25 percent or 50 percent of the pension. Sometimes, it is zero. I have seen that plenty of times.

But let me set all those numbers aside and relate an experience about what an effective retirement blueprint can mean in real-life terms. I met with Bob and Ellen, who came in and asked about what type of strategy they should use for their retirement income. Bob told me he was about to retire and he was not sure whether he should start drawing Social Security right away or wait and draw from his IRA and other investments early on instead. By waiting, he figured, he would receive a larger Social Security benefit later and need less from his investments.

The whole time we were chatting, Ellen was sitting there, clearly anxious. If you have ever seen somebody with the weight of the world on her shoulders, it was Ellen. Her face was pale, her shoulders hunched, and I could see she had a pit in her stomach about this topic of retirement. Bob was asking those questions because they did not have a written plan for how they were going to take their retirement income. He did not know what he should do about his Social Security. He did not know how they should be structuring the distributions from their retirement accounts. Bob and Ellen did not know what strategy they should use with their investments.

> **DIVIDENDS:** Dividends are money or extra shares that a company gives to its shareholders from its earnings.

Fast-forward about ten days. We ended up building a Launch Your Retirement™ Blueprint for them, and they came in to review the plan with me. Bob listened intently, but Ellen was not terribly engaged. What we were discussing mattered to her, of course, but the weight of the world was still on her shoulders. Eventually, we got to the part of our analysis that addressed survivorship income planning.

When I walked through that with Ellen, it was like the weight lifted. Bob was about eight years older than Ellen, so between the two of them, who really needed that plan? Ellen, of course. We outlined a plan that accounted for the income she may need if and when something happened to Bob in the future. Their grandchildren lived on the other side of the country, and she wanted to make sure that she was going to be able to visit her grandkids a couple times a year even as a widow. To see the relief on her face after we had reviewed the survivorship plan was extremely gratifying.

MONEY MANAGEMENT

I cannot leave the topic of income planning without talking about money management. We embrace a holistic, comprehensive approach at Bright Lake. What does that look like? It means pulling together all the pieces of your portfolio so they are working together. It means considering your tax situation today and your tax situation tomorrow. That is going to inform how we build your portfolio to generate income.

A framework I like to use as a reference point is your investment portfolio as compared to a rental property. No matter whether the housing market is up or down, or the value of your investment portfolio is up or down, we want it so that every month you get a check. I like to say, "the rent is due." For example, instead of having a tenant pay you rent, you may have a stock pay you a dividend. Or a bond pays a yield. Those dividends and yields pay out at different timeframes. Maybe it is each quarter, maybe it is every month. Sometimes, it is once a year. What we want is for your portfolio to generate consistent income for you.

Many of my clients have rental properties. They are a reliable source of steady income, but after so many years, my clients typically just do not want to deal with the headaches anymore. They don't want to have to deal with some tenant issue such as a broken pipe over Thanksgiving weekend. The nice thing about a mutual fund, or an exchange-traded fund (ETF), is that it does not call you at 1:00 a.m. when the air conditioner is not working.

Just to clarify the difference, typically, ETFs will track a particular index, sector, commodity, or other assets, but unlike mutual funds, which only trade at the end of each trading day, ETFs can be purchased or sold on a stock exchange during the trading day the same way that a regular stock can.

More and more people are accumulating what I like to call a financial junk drawer over the course of their employment years. The days of going to work for one employer and staying there your entire working life are pretty much gone. You can expect to hold several jobs before you retire. I have had clients who have an old 401(k) from one employer here and an old IRA they rolled over elsewhere. Then they have their current employer plan, and they put some money in a Roth. Maybe a former employer had a small pension, but they cannot find the paperwork. Perhaps there is an inheritance coming at some point.

This is all just spread out. Like that junk drawer. A hodgepodge. They get to this point where they realize, **"We've got to figure out how this comes together."**

That is where my Launch Your Retirement™ Blueprint comes in and why a comprehensive plan to pull all these pieces together to solidify their financial future is so valuable.

Imagine, if you will, an intense game of tug-of-war. On one side, everybody is pulling super hard in the same direction. On the other side, everyone is running around pulling in different directions. Which team is going to win? It is going to be the team pulling in the same direction, of course.

We want to make sure that all your different financial accounts are pulling the rope in the same direction. Otherwise, your portfolio is not going to be able to produce income very well. In fact, it is likely that you will run out of money much sooner than you should have, simply because everybody on the team was not working together.

Now that we have a picture of your income, from all the various sources, my job as a financial advisor is protecting and nourishing your golden goose, so it can continue to provide those golden eggs for as long as you need them. And that's where investment planning, our next pillar, takes center stage.

PILLAR 1 SUMMARY:

1. Transition to Retirement: Income planning helps shift from saving to spending in retirement. Your plan should be unique to your needs, covering essential and lifestyle expenses.

2. Replacing Your Paycheck and Play Check: Ensure your baseline expenses are covered and allocate funds for enjoyable activities, creating a balanced retirement income.

3. Maximizing Social Security: Analyze options to optimize Social Security benefits, which can significantly impact your income.

4. Inflation, Taxes, and Survivorship: Plan for inflation and tax efficiency. Ensure financial security for the surviving spouse by planning for income changes.

ACTION STEPS:

- **Review current and future expenses.**

- **Optimize Social Security decisions.**

- **Include strategies for inflation and taxes.**

- **Plan for spousal financial security.**

PILLAR 2

"THE BIGGEST RISK OF ALL IS
NOT TAKING ONE."

— *MELLODY HOBSON* —

INVESTMENT PLANNING

MANAGING YOUR RISK CAN BE TRICKY

One of Stephen Covey's tidbits of wisdom in his popular book, *The 7 Habits of Highly Effective People*, is to begin with the end in mind. What goal are you trying to achieve? How do you get there?

At Bright Lake, this is where we believe every good plan begins: at the end. The five pillars we build are part of the process of starting with the goal in mind and then reverse engineering from there. Investment planning is the next pillar in building your financial house.

When I talk about investment planning, what I am talking about is investment management itself. How are your assets allocated? We want to make sure that we have the correct asset allocation to properly build your blueprint for retirement.

I have mentioned the golden goose. In our planning process, how do we develop and nurture that golden goose so it can lay those golden eggs reliably and predictably throughout your retirement?

Another way to look at your investment plan is to liken it to a car. In that scenario, your investment plan, the asset allocation, is the engine. Who do you want building and then maintaining your engine? Someone who specializes in that type of car, naturally.

When it comes to your retirement blueprint, you want to make sure that you are working with a financial advisor who concentrates on planning specifically for retirement. There is a big difference between those advisors who help people save money and reach retirement (often called accumulation advisors) versus a retirement advisor—an advisor who focuses on the five pillars of retirement planning.

When considering the "engine" of your retirement blueprint, do you want fuel efficiency? Do you want a 4-cylinder, a V6, or the power of a V8? A pony car like a Mustang or Corvette or Camaro is going to have a lot of horsepower because of the V8, but it is not necessarily optimized for fuel efficiency.

With investment planning, we are constructing the engine that drives the car. Let's say you're buying a used car for your son or daughter. The advice I hear a lot of parents give is, "Let's make sure we have a mechanic do an inspection on the car and the engine, because that's the guts of it." When folks move into retirement and make the transition from saver to spender, when they make the biggest transition of their financial life, it is important to make sure we do an inspection on the engine. Sometimes I will call that a portfolio analysis or a portfolio crash test.

We have got to make sure that you are going to be safe and capable of going through your retirement. I say to my clients, "You are only going to want to retire once, because if you must return to the workforce, it means your golden goose isn't laying sufficient eggs for you. Therefore, you want to make sure that you measure twice and only cut once."

If you look at most retirees, they have built up their assets over a long period of time. Most Americans have a lot of their savings in their employer plan, such as their 401(k). They may have some cash savings as well as their home, either paid off or with equity. As you go through your life and you start to see retirement on the horizon, you may realize, "There's a lot of money here," and you discover that you are now the CEO of a seven-figure enterprise when calculating your total net worth.

Maybe you did it yourself, maybe you worked with a financial advisor. However you reached that seven-figure total, basic math will tell you that a 10 percent wrong decision is a $100,000 mistake, as I mentioned earlier in making that Social Security decision. With so much at stake, it is helpful to have someone come in alongside you as something of a CFO—a chief financial officer—to assist you with important decisions so that you can go through retirement and not have to be worried about making a 10 percent wrong decision.

You also want to make sure that if something happens to you, your spouse is going to be taken care of financially. I had a client who had done all the investment management. When Manuel passed away, his wife, Maria, came to me to pick up the pieces. She had no idea how to manage their money. Luckily, we were able to set her up in excellent shape. But I have seen it many times where we are sitting down with a widow several years after her husband passed and she did not know what to do when he died.

To put it bluntly—and a bit sadly—she was seeking advice from other professionals, but she did not know what questions to ask. As a result, she was in a much worse position financially.

Even if you are that person who has done your planning yourself and really want to have your hands on the wheel, at some point it does start to make sense to let go. If you look at your spouse and ask them if they are comfortable, ready, and capable of managing this, if they are really honest and they're saying no, then you might want to be part of the decision-making process and help determine who they will be working with down the road. That way you can be confident knowing your spouse will not be taken advantage of and what you have worked so hard for won't be squandered.

When you picture that CFO coming alongside you, think of them as a copilot. It is nice to have another pair of well-trained eyes to look at all the gauges in the cockpit so you can land the proverbial retirement airplane.

CHOOSE YOUR ADVISOR WELL

In his bestselling book *Outliers: The Story of Success*, Malcolm Gladwell talks about the 10,000-hour rule. He explains that it takes "10,000 hours of intensive practice to achieve mastery of complex skills." Maybe you have spent years managing your finances and your investments, and you have done well. Perhaps you have even achieved the 10,000 hours necessary to become an expert in the area of personal finance. (I am talking to all my engineers and accountants out there!)

But as the prospect of retirement appears on the horizon—or especially if it is staring you in the face—you will likely reach a point where you have more questions than answers. Are you ready to put in another 10,000 hours to become an expert at managing a retirement plan? After all, you are only going to want to retire once.

This is why I emphasize working with someone who concentrates specifically in the type of planning you need. For folks making the transition to retirement or walking through it, that means finding an advisor who focuses on the five pillars of retirement planning. An advisor who concentrates like this can walk you through the many strategies that can become the framework for your unique retirement blueprint.

So now you might say, "Okay, that makes sense. But, Ted, how do I actually find the right advisor to work with?"

I get this question often and it is a hard question to answer without the proper context. I will include what I believe to be the three most important qualities to look for when hiring your advisor.

> **CONSIDER THIS:**
> Of the 321,000 advisors in the US, according to the US Bureau of Labor Statistics (in 2021), only 15,396—approximately 5 percent—are SEC-registered investment advisors.

1. FIDUCIARY STANDARD OF CARE

When it comes to the management of your investments, I believe your advisor should be held to a fiduciary standard of care, which means they are legally bound to act with your best interests in mind and disclose conflicts of interest to you. It means your interests are put above the interests of the advisor. I believe this allows for a foundation of trust to be built.

Fiduciary is not a job title. It won't appear as a credential after someone's name. It is a standard of care that someone in the field of investment management operates under. Many people can say they are retirement planners, but if they don't have the proper securities license, they are not held to a fiduciary standard of care.

Consider this: Of the 321,000 advisors in the US, according to the US Bureau of Labor Statistics (in 2021), only 15,396—approximately 5 percent—are SEC-registered investment advisors (also known as RIAs or independent advisors), so says the Investment Adviser Association, using 2023 figures. Like a doctor or lawyer, investment advisors have a fiduciary duty and a legal obligation to act in their clients' best interests at all times.

Wouldn't you rather work with a financial advisor who acts in your best interest? Unfortunately, most people don't know the difference.

How can you find out if an advisor must operate with a fiduciary standard of care? Simply ask a prospective advisor if they have any licenses. And then check online to see what each of those credentials truly means. Start your search with the respected FINRA site at brokercheck.finra.org.

2. INDEPENDENT

I believe it is also important to work with an independent firm—in other words, an advisor should be showing you a wide range of investment options, not just a handful. I have seen it before at firms where they get a kickback, or what is called a revenue share, when they select certain financial funds. That means the advisor has a potential conflict of interest and profit incentive to show you or "push" certain funds.

When you work with someone who is an independent advisor, it works much like an independent insurance agent you may buy your auto insurance from. They are not captive so they don't represent a specific company. They represent the client. So they go shop the different options for you and come back with the most competitive price for the coverage you are looking for.

With investments, it is similar. An independent advisor is going to be representing you and looking for the best options available in the market for you.

3. EXPERIENCE

THE FIVE COMPONENTS:

- **Risk**
- **Fees**
- **Volatility Control**
- **Investment Strategy: Income vs. Growth**
- **Longevity Protection**

Finally, work with an advisor who concentrates in the type of planning that you need. We all understand this as it pertains to our medical needs but somehow many of us fail to apply this to our investments. For example, as you get older, you no longer see a pediatrician. If you need to have your heart checked, you are going to talk to a cardiologist.

A family physician is important for general ailments, but when the rubber meets the road, we all know we want to see a specialist.

FIVE COMPONENTS OF INVESTMENT PLANNING

As I mentioned before, I like to view investment planning as the engine that drives your retirement vehicle. Let's take a look at the five components of that engine and then discuss each one in more depth

1. RISK

One of our first steps in crafting a retirement blueprint is to assess your risk tolerance. That will allow us to properly build your asset allocations and decide what securities we are going to hold—essentially, how we are going to build this money machine.

Just for a brief definition, securities are your investments, what you are investing in, whether that is a stock in a company or a credit relationship such as a Treasury bond with the government. In essence, these are your investments or fuel for the engine and where you have placed your money.

People talk a lot about measuring risk. How much risk are you comfortable taking with your securities?

What it comes down to is if you do not get this right, it is easy to end up making an emotional decision with your entire life savings. Here is what I mean: One of my current clients told me that in 2001, with the tech companies flying high, he was taking all this risk getting great returns. When the market cratered and the dot-com bubble burst, Mark just could not take it and he sold low. He thought the tech sector was all going to hell in a handbasket. He suffered tremendous losses by bailing out and selling his securities.

He then built up his investments again, leading up to 2008. Then the economy crashed, and he sold his investments. Low. Big loss. In April 2020, after the financial markets sank, he walked into my office and told me he did the same thing again. You might blame Mark for selling off at bad times, but I have a different perspective: I believe it all happened because the advisor he was working with did not have a good handle on Mark's risk tolerance. They were not properly measuring Mark's ability to handle risk, and his history showed that.

The point is this: Getting your risk tolerance right is significant because, otherwise, bad advice in tough times (and fear) can cost you a lot of money. In his case, Mark lost hundreds of thousands of dollars unnecessarily. When it comes to risk tolerance and long-term thinking with your money, I like to use the analogy of walking up a jagged mountain. The long-term trend is up, but you've got to go up and down, up and down along the way. When you think about risk tolerance, how much "down" along that overall trend of "up" are you comfortable with?

In other words, would it scare you if you lost 10 percent ($10,000) of a $100,000 investment? That is a measure of risk tolerance. If you say, "I'm okay with that level of risk," would you be okay with a 40 percent risk? The answer is unique to each individual.

The bottom line is, when you build your financial house properly, you can weather the ups and downs of the stock market. Some people have cash set aside in annuities or CDs and money market funds, so they might be fine with a higher level of risk.

2. FEES

Roy and Katie worked hard their entire lives to save for their retirement. They had always been mindful of their finances and had sought the advice of an accumulation advisor to help them plan for their golden years.

As they approached retirement, they felt confident in the investments they had chosen and were looking forward to the freedom and relaxation that comes with it. As they sat down to review their portfolio, however, they realized that they had not paid enough attention to the fees associated with their investments. While they had made smart investment choices, the fees they were paying were eating away at their account values and could potentially impact their ability to live the retirement they had planned for.

They were shocked to learn that over the past twenty years, they had paid tens of thousands of dollars in fees that could have been avoided if they had been more mindful of the costs in their portfolio.

Roy and Katie were frustrated and worried. They knew that they needed to take action to ensure their retirement savings would last as long as they needed it. They realized that the fees they were paying were not being charged in a transparent way. I specifically remember one of the things Roy said: "I just don't know what I don't know."

Isn't that the case with so many things in life? It's hard to determine exactly what all the costs are in your portfolio without knowing the right questions to ask. Thankfully, they recognized this before it was too late. They were able to review their portfolio and make changes that reduced their fees, allowing them to keep more of their money working for them.

By being mindful of the fees in their portfolio, Roy and Katie were able to protect their retirement savings and better ensure that they could enjoy their golden years without worrying about their nest egg being eroded by unnecessary expenses.

> **Translation: Paying attention to the small details makes a big difference in the long run.**

Roy and Katie's experience is a reflection of why, for me, the second important aspect of the investment planning pillar is fees. There are all kinds of fees and costs associated with investing. Fees in your investments are a lot like going to the grocery store. You can buy meat there, you can buy fruit, you can buy chips and cereal and bread. But is the name brand of flour worth the extra price when you could buy a house-labeled brand of flour for significantly less? In a similar way, some investment fees are going to be more expensive than others. It is important to be able to determine what is worth paying for and what isn't.

You may find line items on your financial statements that spell out the fees (or you might not be able to identify the fees so easily). You could see items called a transaction fee, management fee platform fee, fund fee, advisory fee, 401(k) administration fee and financial planning fee. Plenty of other items also come right out of your account like a mortality and expense fee, rider fee, sales loads, turnover expenses, and commissions.

Find out what each fee is. When you work with an advisor, you must be able to trust that they are working in your best interest and not overcharging you with fees.

Let's go through different types of fees. The most foundational expense in a portfolio is your expense ratio or your **fund fee**. These are fees that get paid before you ever see an investment return on your fund. This is before you ever pay your advisor or you have paid any transaction fees. If you have a financial fund, whether it is a mutual fund, exchange-traded fund, or a managed fund, if that fund goes up 10 percent, that means you got 10 percent after the fund fee was paid.

If you have a fund fee or an expense ratio that was 50 basis points, or 0.5 percent, then that return, technically, before fees, was 10.5 percent; however, on your statement, it only showed 10 percent because the fee was taken out of performance. That is the fund fee—the most foundational expense in a portfolio. No matter who is managing your funds—an advisor or the company itself—you still pay fund fees.

Often, families we work with do not even know that these fees exist. You can find your fund fees, your expense ratios, in your prospectus. A prospectus is that big, boring legal document that we quickly toss straight into the trash every time we get it in the mail and never look at.

Beyond fund fees, you could also pay **transaction fees**. Depending on the broker you work with, you may pay sales loads, like a front-end load, or a back-end load. For example, a commission may be paid on the front end when buying or paid on the back end when selling. These costs can vary depending on the class of share that is purchased, but I won't go into that much detail here.

You could have what is called a **platform fee**. If, for instance, you are using a certain company's investing platform, they may charge a fee. This is possible with any trading platform. Some are free, some have expenses. Generally, the larger firms—for example Fidelity, Vanguard, and Schwab—are not going to charge you a platform fee if you want to invest money on their platform. Regardless, it is still an important question to ask because all of the decimal points can really add up.

There are also model and **money management fees**. Let's say you have a target 60/40 portfolio and you want to make sure you don't have to think about keeping that in line. You may have a model manager fee, which is beyond your fund fees. Of course, you have your

financial advisory fees. Some of these are rolled in together, but you need to be aware of what the various fees are. There is no such thing as a free lunch: There are costs somewhere, and you need to know what they are.

Let me come back to my grocery analogy: It is helpful at a high level when you think about all the items you can buy, but it is also really valuable when you think about fund costs. Let's say you go to the grocery store and you are looking at buying eggs. Twenty years ago, we would buy eggs and just go home. But now there are all kinds of eggs at the store. You can buy normal eggs, you can buy cage-free eggs, you can buy non-GMO eggs—and any one of these cartons you pick up is going to have a different price. Some are more expensive than the others. Some of them are worth paying more for, but at the end of the day, when you go home and make an omelet, you are eating eggs.

> **VOLATILITY CONTROL:**
> Managing how much an investment's value goes up and down to make it more stable.

What you want to make sure of is that with these different funds that you own, you don't overpay for the same exact thing. I see it all the time. We will look at portfolios, and we'll find that a client may be significantly overpaying for a financial fund when they could get the exact same thing at a fraction of the cost. The broader point about fees is that they are basically termites that eat away at your investment returns from the inside out. Often, people do not realize what is happening until it's too late. Those "termites" can have a huge effect on your long-term return. We want to make sure you do a periodic termite check, where we make sure you know what your expenses are.

3. VOLATILITY CONTROL

The third aspect of investment planning is **volatility control**. That has more to do with your risk capacity, which is how much risk you are able to reasonably take given your time horizon. Risk capacity is distinctly different from risk tolerance. For instance, a seventy-year-old has a much shorter time horizon of life than a thirty-year-old. Thus, managing the ups and downs of your investments accordingly is extremely important.

First and foremost, we need to understand your capacity for risk and then determine how much tolerance for risk you have.

It is not because of fees that folks are getting absolutely lost financially. Nick Murray, a financial services professional and author, cites that more than 80 percent of return is actually driven by investor behavior. That is one of the reasons it is so important to have a good financial advisor. It is why I like to use the analogy of walking up a mountain with a yo-yo. Risk is how much of the down along that overall trend of up a person is comfortable with. If risk is measured incorrectly, the data shows us that these miscalculations have significant consequences.

Risk is hard for people to gauge because they typically get asked, "Are you aggressive, moderately aggressive?" and "Are you moderate, moderately conservative, or conservative?" It is as if you have to put yourself in one of these boilerplate options and you're done. I think it is helpful to give people a framework and quantify risk in terms of dollars. If you are a surfer, how big of a wave are you truly comfortable riding? If you think in terms of a roller coaster, how steep of a drop can you handle?

When we get into retirement, people will sometimes think, "I want to get as high of a rate of return as possible." That is understandable, because it is how they have thought about their money for a long time. But let's think about what the market has been doing recently. There has been a lot of volatility along with rampant inflation.

In baseball terms, if you have reached retirement, do you think you need to swing for the fences and try to hit a home run every time you're at the plate? Do you need as great of an investment return as possible? The truth is, you are much better off from a financial analysis standpoint when you simply start producing income on a consistent basis. You don't want to have these massive swings in your portfolio. This is what I mean when I talk about volatility control. You just want to hit singles consistently. **That is a formula for success in retirement.**

I first met with Don when he was going to sell his business and transition to retirement. As I got to understand his situation, it was clear that he had so much passion for his industry and that despite his long career, his business still had so much untapped potential. The way he talked about it, I could hardly understand why he wanted to sell and retire. What he pointed out was an important lesson we can all learn from.

Don said, "When you first set out to start a new venture, often you do not have much to lose. So you take a large amount of risk with a relatively small amount of money. Later, as a business grows and as wealth is accumulated, you need to change that formula. You cannot always chase the latest and greatest opportunity. You need to instead take a small amount of risk when you have a large amount of money."

He did end up making the decision to sell and take some of his chips off the table. Don put the emphasis on preserving what he had built instead of continuing to chase a higher and higher "number."

I am reminded of a popular Warren Buffett quote. When we think about volatility control and how much risk you are taking, the Oracle of Omaha famously says, "Only when the tide goes out do you discover who's been swimming naked."

Everyone wants great market returns when the markets are good. They are all cool with the risk because they know about risk and reward, and they want the reward. It is in the bad times that we discover who was taking more risk than they should have been.

Are you the investor, like Mark, who sold low just to get out of a sinking market? You are likely taking too much risk if that is the case. We find out who is getting washed out financially or who can't retire or who has to go back to work because they were taking too much risk when the tide goes out.

As the legendary boxer Mike Tyson put it, "Everybody's got a plan until they get punched in the face." We are going to get all these great returns; retirement is going to be easy. Then, boom: A war breaks out, inflation occurs, or 2008 happens, or there is a tech bubble burst. Then what?

Everyone wants a diversified portfolio, and for good reason. But people often do not really think about why that is a good idea. Diversification of your asset allocation and retirement investments, when done correctly, allows you to reduce volatility, which allows your money to work harder for you throughout your retirement by protecting your assets and producing more income. But if you have all or most of your eggs in one basket, and that basket falls sharply, those eggs are going to break—and take your financial health down with it.

4. INVESTMENT STRATEGY: INCOME VS. GROWTH

As we consider how to structure your retirement blueprint, one of the key elements we consider is the dichotomy between what you need to have set aside for income and what you need to have set aside for future growth. Which quickly brings me back to your investment time horizon and your capacity for risk. These questions immediately come to mind:

- **How long is this money going to be invested before it is touched?**
- **Are you already dipping into it?**
- **What expenses do you have each month?**

And we quickly come to the golden question, which in this case is, **"How much of your portfolio do you have set aside for income, and how much have you set aside for growth?"** Depending on your net worth and your needs, your proportion is going to vary drastically.

We can think about how to answer this critical question in several different ways. Sometimes, folks are using all their investment assets to produce the retirement income they need. One way we can think about risk capacity analysis at a high level is by using the Prudent Investor Rule. We take 100 and subtract your age, and that gives you a general target percentage of how much of your portfolio you likely need to set aside for growth. What remains—your age—would be set aside specifically for income.

> **"The two rules of investing are**
> **No. 1: Never lose money. No.2: Never forget Rule No. 1."**
> **-Warren Buffett-**

Using this example, a client who is seventy-five would set aside 25 percent of their investments for growth and use 75 percent to generate income. Of course, this is not a hard-and-fast rule, but a broad guardrail to start planning.

If you are somebody who needs all of their invested assets to live off in retirement, you're probably going to use the Prudent Investor Rule as a starting point. At the end of the day, it all comes back to income and how much income you need. This rule helps provide a starting point, some guardrails, to make sure you are in line with a statement you have likely heard your whole life: "The older you get, the more conservative you get."

Now, to use an extreme example, if you have a $10 million portfolio and you are able to supply your income needs from $2 million of it, then you may only use the Prudent Investor Rule calculation on the smaller portion. Then, measure your risk tolerance for the other $8 million separately. Nuances like this are very important, and that is why I say these things must come together.

If you are a real estate investor who is used to taking big risks throughout life in order to make projects happen and earn big financial rewards, you are going to have a much different risk tolerance than, say, a state employee who has been much more careful with their money because of their modest salary. The real estate investor might not actually be able to afford the amount of risk that they are comfortable with. How much risk they are taking should be governed by their risk capacity. Remember our discussion of risk capacity and risk tolerance.

It comes back to your time horizon for this money. For most people, we think about that in terms of age. If you are seventy, you most likely do not have the thirty years ahead of you to ride the waves of the financial markets like someone who is thirty. I am reminded of another Warren Buffett quotation: "The two rules of investing are No. 1: Never lose money. No. 2: Never forget Rule No. 1."

He is not saying that the financial markets are never going to fluctuate. Realizing unnecessary losses is something you must be very careful with. To assure that doesn't happen, you need to make sure your risk tolerance and your risk capacity are properly balanced.

I will come back to the golden goose analogy. If we are not conscious of your risk capacity and the need for controlling volatility, we could accidentally kill your golden goose, and you could run out of income. If you say, "I am a real estate investor. I have taken a lot of risk, and if I am comfortable with it, that should be okay." Let's say you retire at sixty-eight and the markets are bad. Suddenly, the value of your assets drops rapidly and you'll likely be saying, "I can't lose this money."

Making an emotional decision with your life savings because we did not let risk capacity be another governor on your risk tolerance is one way to really do harm to your golden goose. Let's say you have bad returns early on in your retirement. Your golden goose goes from your initial 100 percent to 50 percent of what you started with. Your goose is only going to be able to lay golden eggs that are half of the size of what they were before. That is why the conversation about risk management and producing income is so intertwined.

I am not seeing enough people—or frankly, enough advisors—account for this scenario. They take a set-it-and-forget-it approach. Your retirement is as unique as your fingerprint, and all the different parameters that apply to your family situation need to be accounted for.

5. LONGEVITY PROTECTION

The final aspect of investment planning that I want to highlight is longevity protection. We need your assets to work as long as possible. We do not need you running out of money. People are living longer now than they ever have before. That is why I often belabor my point about some of these set-it-and-forget-it strategies.

Take Social Security for example. When Social Security was established, most people didn't live long enough to collect because the average life expectancy was lower than the age of eligibility for Social Security. With improvements in nutrition and healthcare, our grandmas and grandpas were living into their golden years, and retirement lasted ten or fifteen years or longer.

As long as you had a reasonable amount in your savings account, there was not a lot of room for error in a ten- to fifteen-year timeframe. You could get away with a simple strategy. But people are now living for twenty to thirty years after they retire. Factors such as asset allocation and how much you are paying in fees come into the equation very quickly. **You need to make sure that your money can last as long as you will.**

Let's consider how long you might live. According to the Society of Actuaries, if you have already reached age sixty-five today, you might live to eighty-seven if you are a male and eighty-nine for females. In other words, you have very good odds of living into your late eighties.

And if you are married, statistics show that the chance of one of you living to the age of ninety-seven is 25 percent. If you retire at sixty-five, your retirement money will need to last more than thirty years. That means the decisions you make about your money have significant ramifications over longer periods of time.

Over the course of time, inflation creates a lot of risk as it slowly erodes your buying power, as discussed earlier. That is why longevity protection is so important. And as difficult as a conversation about spousal income planning and survivorship income planning may be, it is highly likely that spouses will not pass away at the same time. If one spouse, let's say, passes away at seventy-eight, and the other passes at ninety-two, that would mean your spousal income plan would be in place for more than a decade.

If you need $1,000 a month to cover expenses and then suddenly a spouse passes away, then their Social Security vanishes because only the higher of the two Social Security payments continues. That is a huge difference in income that needs to be accounted for. A burden that your investments have to bear.

Ultimately, we need to make sure that the engine is built by the proper mechanic with the proper strategy so you have longevity protection. That means managing risk capacity and volatility, minimizing fees, and ensuring you have the proper mix of investments and financial tools in your retirement toolbelt. The right balance will protect your golden goose for as long as you need her.

PILLAR 2 SUMMARY:

1. Begin with the End in Mind: Investment planning involves managing your assets to ensure a stable retirement. Think of your investment plan as the "engine" driving your financial "vehicle."

2. Choosing the Right Advisor: Select an advisor specializing in retirement planning, who acts in your best interest (fiduciary), is independent, and has the necessary experience to guide you.

3. Five Components of Investment Planning:

1. *Risk:* Understand your risk tolerance.

2. *Fees:* Be aware of all fees.

3. *Volatility Control:* Manage ups and downs in the market.

4. *Investment Strategy*: Balance income and growth.

5. *Longevity Protection:* Plan to make your assets last.

ACTION STEPS:

- **Assess your risk tolerance and ensure it matches your retirement strategy.**

- **Review and minimize investment fees.**

- **Develop a balanced investment strategy for income and growth.**

- **Plan for longevity and protect your financial assets.**

PILLAR 3

"THE HARDEST THING IN THE WORLD TO UNDERSTAND IS THE INCOME TAX."

— *ALBERT EINSTEIN* —

TAX PLANNING

YES, UNCLE SAM IS IN YOUR POCKET

Retirement planning is like baking a cake. Tax planning is one of the key ingredients of that proverbial cake. It supports and improves the planning pieces I have covered so far: income planning and investment planning. Think of tax planning as yeast that helps a cake rise as it bakes in the oven.

When it comes to your investments, I believe any comprehensive retirement plan must include a clear strategy for reducing tax liabilities. Not that you can completely avoid paying taxes, but why share more of your hard-earned dollars with Uncle Sam than you have to?

I like to talk about asset location when I discuss tax planning with my clients and with audiences when I speak to groups. What do I mean by this? Let's start by asking some questions: What kind of diversification do you want in your portfolio? What mix of investments do you want to have? Which asset classes? That is called asset allocation.

Not nearly enough advisors are talking about the important distinction between the two. Let me explain.

ASSESSING ASSET ALLOCATION VERSUS LOCATION

Asset location questions sound like this: What kind of tax buckets are you in? What kind of tax levers do we have to work with in advising you? Do you have all your savings in just a 401(k)? Or do you also have your savings in a Roth IRA or a Roth 401(k), where all the growth is tax-free and you do not have to pay taxes on every dollar you pull out? Do you have not only a 401(k), but just a taxable brokerage account—a taxable account where you have paid taxes on the principal where you are only subject to capital gains, whether short-term capital gains or long-term capital gains?

Having a balance of these buckets is going to put you in a position to win, instead of being put under the gun or forced into a much higher bracket than you should have to be. In a higher tax bracket, you pay more in taxes.

The three-bucket strategy of efficient asset location is this. A taxable bucket, a tax-deferred bucket, and an income tax-free bucket. My personal favorite being the last of the three—tax-free. With the proper balance of each, you set yourself up with the unique ability to legally manipulate your tax rate and "name your price" when it comes to sending checks to our favorite taxing uncle.

TAX BUCKETS CREATE TAX OPTIONS

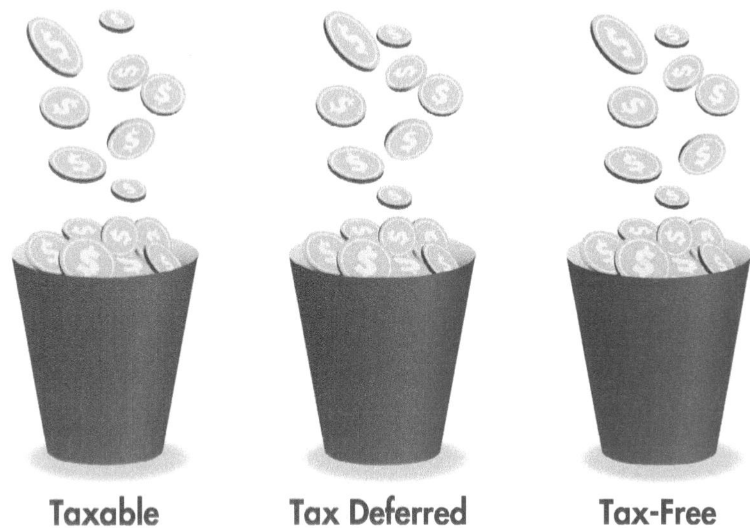

Just for clarification, money put into traditional 401(k) or IRA plans are tax deferred. You pay taxes when you take the money out. Money put into Roth 401(k) or Roth IRAs is money you have already paid taxes on, so when you take the money out, you pay no taxes, even on the growth. The 401(k) plans are administered through employers. The IRA plans are investment devices you direct yourself. Have I totally confused you now?

When most people think about tax planning, it's usually about April of each year and limited to when they file their taxes. At least throughout their earning years, that's where tax planning stops. They talk to their CPA at the end of the year and try to get some tax advice. That is the CPA's job: to save them money on taxes today. Unbeknownst to you, they leave it up to you to think about your taxes twenty and thirty years from now.

And that's where **holistic financial planning** comes in.

What typically happens is people show up at retirement, and they say, "Whoa, we have all this money," which in and of itself is great. It is one of the goals we have as we save. But they quickly realize, "Oh, my gosh, if I want to spend some of that money, there is a significant tax burden. Why?" And they ask themselves (or me), "What could I have done earlier to save instead of having to send such big checks to Washington?"

Ideally, that's the question to ask before you reach retirement. The second best time, to ask it, however, is now.

If you are trying to save money on taxes in the short term and during your savings years, you're going to make pretax contributions. That means you will get a deduction during your savings years. That is a good thing. Tax-deferred growth is what occurs when you contribute pretax dollars. But when you retire, the IRS says, "It is time to pay the piper. There is no such thing as a free lunch." Uncle Sam is trying to get what is his.

> It's perfectly fine to pay Uncle Sam. It's not okay to leave him a tip. We all know it is not just about how much you make; it is about how much you keep.

We all see headlines talking about retirement expenses increasing, and it is easy to point to inflation. But this may surprise you: The largest expense in retirement for most retirees is taxes.

Here is an example: If you want $100,000 in income for twenty-five years during retirement, that's $2.5 million in total. If you take even just a 20 percent effective tax rate, which I would argue is low when we account for federal and state taxes, the amount you are going to pay over time is $500,000—that's a half-million dollars in taxes. That is a massive number. It's perfectly fine to pay Uncle Sam. It's not okay to leave him a tip. We all know it is not just about how much you make; it is about how much you keep.

Tax planning takes a financial plan from good to great and leaves you more you can spend month to month or keep in your nest egg. Why is that? The value of smart tax strategy compounds the other aspects of good planning. We financial planners talk a lot about the value of compounding when we think about investing. The goal is to squeeze as much juice out of the orange as possible. With a great tax plan, you get significantly more out of the same exact plan simply because you are keeping more. Again, it is not about how much you make, it's about how much you keep.

As a financial advisor, our performance is often measured down to the third decimal point—1,000th of a percent. When we are talking about fees, we are looking at the total difference between fees, say, the difference between 1 percent or 2 percent in fees. When we are talking about effective planning from a tax standpoint, the difference could mean paying 30 percent in taxes or 10 percent. We are talking about swings of 10 to 15 percentage points when it comes to how much the retiree is actually keeping. That is why I say it compounds the value of the other parts of planning.

EFFECTIVE STRATEGIES FOR TAX PLANNING

I consider tax planning one of the core tenets of solid financial planning. Let's say you have a fine financial plan—that's like a good fire burning. If you want to throw gasoline on it and really make it take off, add good tax planning to it. Especially when it comes to IRA planning or planning with 401(k) money, if you are not careful and you do not plan around taxes, you end up being the frog that gets boiled in the pot. It gets to be too late to plan for tax savings if you wait too long.

This happens all the time for retirees. I see it on a weekly basis. If you find yourself reading this and realize you do not yet have a tax plan, I can't emphasize enough the importance of getting started as soon as possible. Especially if you are early on in your retirement planning.

If you are already retired, I am not saying that you don't have a lot of time for planning, it's just that the closer you get to the age for taking required minimum distributions (RMDs), the harder it is to plan around it. If you are sixty-five and reading this book, it is time to start planning around RMDs. If you are sixty-eight, the urgency is even higher, so use the time you have to your advantage.

For most of you reading this who have not already started taking RMDs, as of the time of this writing, they are set to begin at age seventy-three. From then on, the IRS requires you to take a minimum distribution amount from your IRAs. The amount you are required to withdraw (and pay taxes on) is based on the amount you have in the IRA.

Bucket 1:	Bucket 2:	Bucket 3:
Tax-deferred bucket. Money goes in before taxes.	Tax-free bucket. Taxes are already paid on this money.	Taxable account. Only pay tax on the gains.

That's why I offer the three-bucket strategy. Let's take a closer look. First, we have our pretax bucket or tax-deferred bucket, meaning money goes in before taxes. You get a tax deduction when you put money into 401(k)s or IRAs. The amount grows on a tax-deferred basis. When you pull the money out, it is taxed as income. That is what most Americans do through a traditional 401(k) or a traditional IRA.

Take a look at the tax-free bucket, such as a Roth IRA or a Roth contribution to a 401(k). You put money into that bucket that you have already paid taxes on. All the growth is tax-free. The taxes have been paid on the principal. When you pull money out—the principal and the ensuing growth come to you tax-free.

Then you have a third bucket, which is called a taxable account, where you've paid taxes on the principal and only pay taxes on any gains. An example would be if you decided to invest money that you had in your checking account. Let's say you buy Apple stock in a brokerage account (and remember you are also paying fees on the brokerage account). If the new Apple iPhone goes crazy and the stock goes up, then you have a gain. If you sell the stock, you capture that gain and you must pay capital gains tax. If you sell within a year of buying the stock, it qualifies as a short-term capital gain (which is taxed as ordinary income, and the tax rates for ordinary income are higher than a long-term capital gain). If you sell a year or more after you bought the stock, long-term capital gains tax rates apply. It works the same way as buying and selling real estate property.

We at Bright Lake genuinely believe that it is wrong for you to pay more than your fair share of taxes. We help you put on your superhero cape and fight the enemy that is excessive taxation. With the proper planning, you get to name your price when it comes to the taxes that you pay.

When we think about tax planning, we can boil it down to two things: **What does your situation look like? In other words, what is the mix of accounts you have? And then what strategies can you use? What are your options for implementation?**

To get those answers, though, we need to ask more questions. What is going on in your world? We must assess the nature of your current holdings. What kind of tax buckets do you already have?

Another way to look at it is what tools do you have in your tool belt already? What tax buckets do you have available to use? What are we going to need to have a tax-efficient retirement plan?

People commonly pose the question, "Am I going to have enough to retire?" Before we can answer that, we need to know what you have already. From an advisor's standpoint, we want to know if a client has qualified accounts or non-qualified accounts. The distinction is which accounts qualify for a tax advantage. If you have a million dollars in your IRA, or a million dollars in your 401(k), do you really have a million dollars? If you take it all out, let's just assume a 25 percent tax rate, you would actually only have $750,000. That is a substantial difference to account for.

There are two types of tax-advantaged accounts: pretax advantaged accounts and post–tax-advantaged accounts. As I mentioned earlier, 401(k) accounts are examples of pretax advantage accounts. A post–tax-advantaged account would be a Roth contribution to your 401(k) or a contribution to a Roth IRA. It is an important distinction, because we will need to know how much of the money we pull out of your accounts is taxable and how much is not subject to any tax.

Let's look at the names of the accounts impacted by this again. The qualified bucket would include your 401(k), your 403(b), or your IRA. Your post-tax qualified tax-advantaged accounts will be your Roth 401(k) and your Roth 403(b). That is two buckets, pretax and post-tax.

The third bucket is any taxable account. This is where you have paid taxes on the principal. If we invest, it grows and is only subject to capital gains taxes on the growth itself. Capital gains are broken down into two categories: short term and long term. Short-term capital gains happen within a twelve-month period. To use the stock purchase example again, if you buy some Apple stock and sell it at a profit six months later, that is a short-term capital gain.

- **Short-term capital gains** *are subject to ordinary income tax rates. So whatever taxes you pay on your income, that is what your short-term capital gains are subject to.*
- **Long-term capital gains** *occur if you sell a position after twelve months have passed. Those long-term gains are subject to separate tax rates, often more advantageous (lower) than the income tax rates that short-term gains are subject to.*

Ramsey Solutions conducted the largest study of millionaires that has ever been done by studying over 10,000 of them. They found the average American millionaire is minted because of the value of their home plus the value of their 401(k). Reading between the lines, it is not hard to conclude most Americans save money primarily in a 401(k) or an IRA. Obviously, having a nice amount of savings in an IRA or 401(k) is a good thing. The problem is, when you have all your savings in a 401(k) or an IRA, you eventually must take distributions.

When that happens, it can be a bittersweet burden because of how much of a tax liability they are.

Most folks do fine taking systematic, scheduled distributions every month in retirement. Taxes are withheld automatically, and after a while you hardly notice it. But guess what? Retirement comes with unexpected expenses. For example, you need a new car. If you only have a 401(k) or IRA to pull that money from, you're suddenly considering taking out a loan on the car.

> **Required Minimum Distribution:**
> **The minimum amounts you must withdraw from your retirement accounts each year once you reach a certain age.**

When you have a net worth that is substantial enough to be able to cover this kind of purchase, you must be careful. Why? In order to buy a $50,000 vehicle, you have to pull $70,000 or $75,000 from your IRA. That money counts as income, on top of your standard monthly distributions. It is likely that a lump sum distribution like this will vault you into a new tax bracket with a higher tax rate. Taking your grandkids on a big family trip could do the same thing. Certainly, this situation comes up when you start to think about healthcare expenses and long-term care expenses as well (and I'll talk about that pillar in the next chapter). If you aren't careful, you can get backed into a corner with taxes.

Facing this predicament and calling it bittersweet is the nice way of putting it. Otherwise, call it what it is: extremely frustrating. You feel as if you are getting taken advantage of because you do not have flexibility. When you first retire, you are going to be doing a lot more activity that has a price tag. We call them your go-go years for a reason—because you are going places and doing things you always wanted to do. But these tax burdens can put a governor, if you will, on how much you can go and do. From there, you can end up in a situation you don't even realize is coming: a tax buzz saw headed straight for you once RMDs begin at age seventy-three.

RMD stands for required minimum distribution. Let me explain what happens. The IRS looks at the value of all your qualified, non-Roth accounts, and they will force you to distribute a certain portion of the value of those accounts based on your age. There are many rules about where you can take the RMDs from, and I won't go into them here. Ultimately, the IRS mandates you withdraw a certain portion, which all counts as taxable income. That amount you are required to take increases each year. If you are not careful, you will end up looking at your spouse in your late seventies and early eighties and wonder why on earth you are paying so much in taxes.

COMMON TAX PLANNING MISTAKES

A lot of people who have most of their investments in an IRA or a 401(k) and do not diversify any of their asset allocation or location are likely going to be the frog that gets slowly boiled in the pot and does not realize it until it's too late.

I will offer an example, but first I want to talk about the three phases of retirement that I hinted at before. You have your go-go years when you first retire, when you are traveling and checking off the items on your bucket list that you just never got around to while you were working. Then, for most people, by the time they hit their mid-seventies, they're in their slow-go years, where you're still doing things but not as often or as far away. Then in your eighties, most have reached the no-go years where you simply stay home more without the desire to travel and move around like you once did.

As much as this is nature's way of slowing us down as we get older, it also coincides with most people's preferences. You have gotten to do things and savor life in wonderful ways, and so your desire to go isn't as much as it used to be. That is a practical way to look at your retirement years.

Now to that example I promised. Brian and Cindy are squarely in the third phase of their life, their retirement. You can think about life in phases. Your first phase is learning; you are going to school and dependent on others. In the second phase of your life, others are dependent on you, and you are trying to reach financial independence yourself. The third phase of life is really where you reach that point of financial independence and you are now getting to savor life and give back by teaching others the skills that made you successful. I am going to define this as late seventies and early eighties.

Brian and Cindy are sitting next to each other in rocking chairs on the porch, looking across their yard as two birds are chasing one another in circles. They are savoring the beauty of life. They go inside after they finished their morning cup of coffee, and they see a letter on the counter that came in the mail. It's from the IRS, and guess what? They owe $8,573 in taxes.

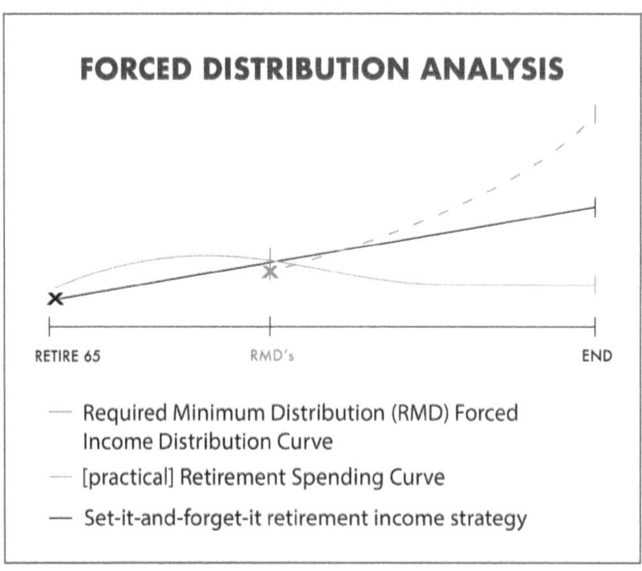

This is the situation I see a lot of folks run into if they don't do any IRA planning. It's what I mean when I say we don't want you to be that frog boiling in the hot water of taxes. There is a timeline when it comes to retirement: Let's say you're able to retire at sixty-five, so that would be the beginning of the timeline. Obviously, the end of your life would be the end of the timeline. For the sake of this discussion, we will call it age 100. Most advisors think about retirement spending simply in a linear way. Today, you need $6,500 a month plus inflation every year. Account for that, and we're done—in other words, you need $6,500 a month today plus whatever the rate of inflation is. Next year, you are going to need $6,500 plus whatever inflation is, and then we'll keep going. That is the solid line in my example.

The solid line would represent a set-it-and-forget-it way to think about retirement income. I'm not saying that's bad, necessarily. But we need to balance the hard science of planning with the practical art of it. The way we see retirees spend money is more like the dotted line in this graphic. Retirees have their go-go years and then they have their slow-go years and then they have their no-go years.

In my first example, the solid line, at the end of your life, you are spending more money every single month than you ever have in your whole life. Anyone who really thinks about that in a practical sense understands that that is probably not going to be the case. Practical retirement spending looks a lot more like the dotted curve. It is what I would call the retirement curve of spending.

The problem with that practical curve is that you can quickly see how people end up like Brian and Cindy, owing the IRS extra money. Why? When you start to think about the slow-go years, required minimum distributions kick in (as noted in the graphic as a soaring dashed line).

Every year, you are forced to take a larger and larger percentage of your investment accounts as distributions, which creates more and more taxable income. At first, you do not really notice it. You're likely spending more than the minimum requirement anyway. But by the time your late seventies and early eighties roll around, you are thinking, "I do not need to take this money out. I want to let it keep growing." Yet Uncle Sam says, "No, you have to take it as income." That ratchets you up into a higher and higher tax rate.

This is where planning with only a rule of thumb really hurts you. And it's another reason we believe so much in the importance of having a retirement blueprint to follow that's unique to you. How many times have you heard, "Don't worry about taxes in retirement, you're going to be in a lower income tax bracket then anyway"? This is something I hear far too often from advisors and even from CPAs. You often hear that phrase each year when you go to file your taxes—at about the same time you make your annual IRA contribution.

The problem is this: Often, it is a false statement. Once you retire, you are going to have much more time on your hands than you do today. You are going to want to go and enjoy yourself the way you always thought about doing in your golden years. Do you really think suddenly you are going to be living on a shoestring budget—living on less than you did while you were working? Of course not. The problem only then compounds further once those RMDs really start to hurt in your no-go years.

I am passionate about this. I really do believe it when I say it is wrong for you to pay more than your fair share of taxes. I consider this scenario something of a bait and switch. People get into a tough situation because their tax preparer asks them during their savings years to save taxes in the short term. That is a good thing. But nobody's sitting there looking out for their long-term tax interest. Then here comes Ted as a financial advisor, trying to pick up the pieces and make sure you have balanced options when it comes to your investment tax strategy in retirement.

> **CAPITAL GAINS:**
>
> **The profits made from**
>
> **selling an investment for more than you paid for it.**

When it comes to tax planning, we want to think about your IRA in a very important way. We don't want you to be over allocated, from an asset location standpoint to an IRA, because of the lack of flexibility that I was talking about earlier. That can put you right squarely in the crosshairs of the tax buzz saw that is headed straight for you when required minimum distributions start.

Let's explore a variety of tax strategies: tax-free, tax-deferred, and taxable money strategies. We will be layering tax strategy onto your income plan. As I mentioned earlier, a lot of advisors talk about asset allocation—diversification. Not nearly enough talk about asset location, which are the tax buckets, the tax levers that we can use for retirement planning.

Let's say you have that pretax account, that IRA or 401(k). Let's say you have a tax-free Roth account. You also have a taxable account, whether it is an individual account, a joint account, or a trust account. Where would we put which funds and how much?

Let's discuss growth assets. If you are going to be aggressive and try to grow money—perhaps with some technology stocks or emerging market stocks or small-cap stocks (sometimes people would put large-cap stocks in here, too, but let's just use those three to start with)—I would suggest putting this money in the account where all the growth is tax-free: your Roth account.

When you are thinking about your asset allocation through the lens of asset location, we're going to put the right things in the right places. **The high growth is going to be in the place where the growth gets all the tax-free benefit.** If you are going to look at what you might put in a pretax account, like your IRA or your traditional 401(k), it's likely going to be the stocks that pay dividends. The dividends are taxed the same way as income, so you may as well put them in that account. Your high-yield bonds would be great to put in a pretax, traditional IRA, because the bond yield is taxable just like the distribution from an IRA is taxable. We are matching like-to-like when we do that.

What would you put in the third bucket, the non-qualified account, the taxable account? Perhaps a tax-free municipal bond, where the income it generates is tax-free, or maybe large-cap stocks that grow well but don't pay as much in dividends, and financial funds that don't have a lot of turnover. That means they are not going to generate a lot of capital gains. You can still get growth, but you are not going to get hammered with taxes.

You might also simply put cash in there and have a stable value focus, such as a money market account that earns a couple percentage points of interest per year. As you can see, asset allocation and diversification are most efficient when looking through the lens of asset location.

There are also Roth conversion strategies. If you are Brian and Cindy from my previous example, if you are the person staring right at the tax buzz saw, if you are the person who does not want to be the frog that gets boiled in the pot and you have the majority of your savings in your 401(k) and your IRA, then we need to start to create other tax buckets. We probably need to consider converting some money from your IRA to your Roth IRA, or creating one if you do not have one, which means taking some of that money and paying the tax on it now so you can get it into a Roth, where all future growth is tax-free. In a Roth, there are no required minimum distributions, and they get inherited tax-free.

When it comes to considering Roth IRA conversions, it's important to be sensitive to your income situation. If you are in your working years and you are making $150,000 a year or so, you may think, "I won't worry about taxes, because I'll be in a lower tax bracket once I retire."

A lot of folks I talk to these days want to maintain the same income that they have had throughout their earnings years. Or some of them even want a little bit more because they need to be able to meet their monthly needs that they always have, but they also want to go and do more of what excites them. It's not particularly likely that you're going to have a lower tax rate if you're trying to do more, unless you have a good tax plan and an effective strategy for your tax situation.

Another aspect of tax planning is **tax loss harvesting**. What is that? When invested well, over the course of time, your investment accounts tend to increase in value. But, as we all know, the market has its swings. As you recall, I described those swings as walking up a mountain with a yo-yo. When you have positions in an account that have depreciated in value, you may decide to sell those and repurchase something else. At the same time, you may also sell a position that has appreciated in value. You are offsetting the gain with the loss that you harvested.

Let's say that you're not in retirement but you're nearing retirement. Using a strategy like this over time would allow you to end up increasing the principal basis of your investment so long as you offset gains with losses you harvested. That is a valuable strategy. If you are already in retirement, you just created potential income with no tax consequence. Your non-qualified account suddenly just worked a lot like your Roth IRA. That is why tax loss harvesting is so valuable.

THE TRUTH ABOUT IRA'S

Beyond being able to take advantage of tax loss harvesting, having a standard taxable investment account (that would be an individual brokerage account or trust account) outside of your typical retirement accounts (which are the 401(k)s and IRAs) also provides flexibility if you want to retire before the age of fifty-nine-and-a-half. Why?

That IRA, despite it being pretax, is not advantaged until you are fifty-nine-and-a-half. Any withdrawals taken before that date are penalized. If you were to take a distribution from your IRA before you reach the age of fifty-nine-and-a-half, you would not only have to pay taxes but also pay a 10 percent penalty. If you want to retire before you reach fifty-nine-and-a-half, you need a good nonqualified taxable account to serve as a bridge account to help cover your needs between your early retirement age and when you turn fifty-nine-and-a-half. **If you want a key to being able to retire early, it is having one of these accounts in place.**

Unfortunately, outside of very specific provisions, you are in shackles with your IRA until fifty-nine-and-a-half. You need a bridge account to give yourself flexibility. Maybe you want to take out a lump sum to buy a vehicle in order to avoid a loan in retirement. Perhaps you want to take your family on a big trip or buy some toys such as a boat or an ATV. Often, folks want to be able to go and do some of these things, so having a place to pull from that is appropriate and tax-efficient is important. Otherwise, your hands are tied. Are you not going to do the fun stuff in retirement that you have always wanted to do and thought about doing throughout your working years just because of the tax situation? That would be ridiculous.

I was talking with some of our clients, Len and Malia, recently and our conversation really put this into perspective for me. Len said "Ted, Malia and I have talked about the future for so long. We've always said that someday we'll get to go and do this or get to enjoy that. Finally, we're done saying that." He told me, "Now, we are living in the somedays."

Having a bridge account allows you to not have restrictions when you set out to do those things you have always wanted to do—the much-talked-about bucket list.

Beyond your bucket list, if you are charitably inclined, there is also a tremendous opportunity for strategic gifting. If your goal is to strategically give away your accumulated wealth, you may employ many strategies depending on the type of account. I will stick with a nonqualified account example since that was the point I just made.

A donor-advised fund can provide a large tax write-off all at once. Let's say you bought $1,000 worth of stock and now it's worth $25,000. If you sell it, you will have to pay taxes on a capital gain of

$24,000—probably a long-term gain given how much it went up in value. Instead of selling it and dealing with the tax burden, you could instead donate that money to a donor-advised fund, which will allow you to get a charitable write-off for the full amount and then split up the donations to charities of your choice over time. It can be a valuable option if you need or are looking for a tax write-off.

Another way to go might be a **qualified charitable distribution**, or QCD. Let's say you have RMDs coming in and you didn't plan for them ahead of time from a tax standpoint. You could allocate all or a part of that distribution to a charity or a church, giving you a one-for-one wash on income received if you did not need that money.

Using QCDs could be an ideal strategy to sidestep the tax buzz saw that I keep mentioning. If you already have an efficient plan in place and you are more charitably inclined, it could be a natural way for you to give in a fashion that puts you in control so you do not feel backed into a corner by the potential tax challenges of an RMD.

These options all tie in with tax-efficient income strategies. This is where a holistic approach is so important. For many financial advisors, tax is a four-letter word. There are a lot of reasons for that. Some of my colleagues in the financial world just do not want to dive in and become an expert on investment tax strategies. They simply want to do investment management, so they avoid the topic, rather than focus on becoming a holistic financial planner.

You may think, "Well, my CPA handles my taxes for me." But there is a big difference between a tax preparer and somebody who does tax strategy. A lot of CPAs intend to be a tax strategist. Yet, in a practical sense, most of them end up being the former—a tax preparer. They want to take your information and file the taxes. They are simply going to file what you give them, more or less. I have a lot of sympathy for them because that's hard work handling so many tax returns every year. It could be in the hundreds or even a thousand or more.

But this is where holistic financial planning comes into place because, especially in retirement, **you need a custom approach that is specific to you**. Most of the people I sit down with recognize this difference. We cannot only be thinking about this tax year; we need to be thinking about taxes ten, fifteen, or twenty or more years down the road.

You may have heard of the three-legged stool of financial professionals. One leg is your investment manager. Sometimes people call this their financial advisor, but too often these advisors really deal just with investments rather than holistic planning. The second leg is your CPA, who files your taxes. They are not really doing strategies; they are just filing the paperwork. Then you have your estate planning attorney, who created your family's trust. If you have a higher net worth—say $2 million or more—this arrangement is reasonably common.

You can think of this arrangement as a triangle, with you in the middle. You are typically expected to be the quarterback among all these people. You go to your financial advisor and say, "Should we do some Roth conversions?"

"Oh, yeah, that can be valuable," the advisor says. "Let's think about doing that. Why don't you go ask your CPA what they think?"

Then you ask your CPA what their perspective is, but it's tax time, and the CPA is really busy and takes a while to get back to you.

"I think that could make sense," your CPA says eventually. "But you just repositioned things in your trust. Let's check with your estate attorney just to make sure it still makes sense."

Then you talk to your estate planner. Everybody has their fingers pointed at one another—and after some time passes, nothing gets done.

Why?

Because you don't actually have somebody in your corner who's doing holistic planning. You must be the quarterback trying to make things happen among a group of people who don't really talk to one another. Do you want that responsibility?

At Bright Lake, we work with you to fit in the middle of that triangle, so you do not have to be the quarterback alone. We have a CPA on retainer, and we keep an estate planning attorney on retainer. Of course, we are handling the investment management. This allows us to come to you and say, "Is this something that you want to do and take advantage of as a strategy? We think it could be valuable to you."

Our holistic approach explores ways to have a flexible income strategy. What you do not want is a single-bucket income strategy, because then you are just tied to one thing—your IRA, for example. Ideally, we have some buckets to work with. Let's say you have an IRA and a Roth IRA. If you take all of your distributions from an IRA—say $60,000 a year—that is $60,000 in taxable income. But if you pulled half from a Roth IRA, and half from a traditional IRA, guess what? You still have $60,000 total, but you are only paying tax on $30,000. Even if you just leave that static at 50/50 throughout retirement, you are cutting your taxable income in half and keeping more money in your pocket.

Jim and Becky came to us about a year after they retired. They were excited because it seemed like everything was on track for them. They went on their first big trip, enjoying themselves, feeling the breeze of the ocean, looking at the palm trees, sipping mai tais and margaritas on the beach.

They got back from Mexico and there was a notice from Medicare about surcharges. Suddenly, their Medicare costs were going to go from about $150 a month to over $350 a month, ultimately because their distributions were all coming from an IRA. The same Medicare coverage was going to cost them hundreds more a month simply because they did not have a tax-efficient structure for their income. What it meant was that they would be keeping less of their money because now they would be charged more for other things. It comes all the way back to the main point I made at the beginning of this chapter: **It is not about how much you make; it is about how much you keep.**

The final point I want to make is essentially a culmination of the other aspects of tax planning that I have highlighted. This occurs when we layer the different aspects of planning on top of one another to get a compounded effect and that is a tax-efficient legacy plan. We want you to leverage your money to squeeze as much juice out of the orange of life as possible, and, at the end, we want you to be able to leave as many tax-free dollars to your beneficiaries as you can. That is the culmination of a good tax strategy.

> **"It's not about how much you make; it's about how much you keep. "**

If you want to leave money to your children and grandchildren, that's all part of your retirement planning. But you must set yourself up for success first. It is not an either/or, it's a both/and.

Tax planning can seem like an afterthought when it comes to your retirement and your legacy. But it shouldn't be. Careful planning is vital. I am not talking about the difference in a couple decimal points of fee savings here. I am talking about huge tax bracket changes. Paying more than your fair share in taxes is not a good idea. As I have said, it is fine to pay Uncle Sam. It is not okay to leave him a tip.

We do not want the tax tail to wag the investment dog. Tax planning is an advanced strategy that you need to layer on top of sound financial fundamentals. A good income plan and a strong investment management plan need to be in place before a tax plan can do its best work for you.

PILLAR 3 SUMMARY:

1. Essential Ingredients: Tax planning is crucial for a comprehensive retirement plan, reducing liabilities and enhancing income and investments.

2. Three-Bucket Strategy: Diversify across taxable, tax-deferred, and tax-free accounts to manage taxes efficiently and maintain flexibility.

3. Avoid Tax Pitfalls: Plan early to prevent unexpected taxes, especially with required minimum distributions (RMDs).

4. Holistic Approach: Integrate tax planning with income, investment, and estate planning to maximize what you keep.

ACTION STEPS:

- **Assess your tax situation and asset locations.**

- **Use a diversified tax strategy for withdrawals.**

- **Start planning early to minimize RMD impacts.**

- **Coordinate with a holistic advisor.**

PILLAR 4

"OFTEN WHEN YOU THINK YOU'RE AT THE END OF SOMETHING, YOU'RE AT THE BEGINNING OF SOMETHING ELSE."

— FRED ROGERS —

HEALTHCARE PLANNING

PUT THE CARE, NOT THE COST,
IN YOUR HEALTH COVERAGE

At Bright Lake, we consider healthcare planning to be part of the strategy behind mitigating risk within your overall plan. Folks are familiar with the concept of mitigating risk within the context of their investments by diversifying their portfolios. So healthcare planning—the fourth pillar for building a sound financial house—is another area where mitigating risk is an important consideration.

In the previous chapter, I talked about how taxes are one of the biggest costs for retirees. Healthcare expenses are another potentially massive cost for retirees. If you do not plan for healthcare costs, you run a huge risk of having to tap into your nest egg and distribute funds from taxable sources such as an IRA or a 401(k). Depending on when you must do that in your retirement arc, withdrawing those sums can thrust you into a bad place.

> **"The cost of healthcare is rising."**
> **Do those headlines scare you?**

I liken it to peeling back the layers of the onion. We go through income planning, we go through investment planning, we go through tax planning, and you start to say, "Ted, how much more can we be planning for?" Then we get to the next piece, healthcare planning, which is yet another important aspect of planning. Honestly, folks can be intimidated by that.

You wonder, "When are we going to get to the bottom of all this?" If you are doing all the management yourself, you start asking plenty of questions. You may be savvy at handling investment management, but what about an income plan, a tax plan, a healthcare plan or a long-term care plan?

As is true with so many things in life, you don't know what you don't know. If you are doing it yourself and you make a 10 percent mistake, as I have emphasized throughout this book, with, say, $1 million, the miscalculation will cost you six figures.

That is why it's so helpful to have a proverbial chief financial officer alongside you to help you make these financial decisions and put all these other pieces into place. Even if you do not have a substantial retirement nest egg, assistance from an advisor can be valuable. **I would even go so far as to use the word crucial.**

Data from Gallup indicate that 44 percent of baby boomers are projected to lack adequate income for their basic retirement and healthcare expenses. That is nearly half of the largest pool of retirees in the nation's history!

Considering that sobering statistic, what I am about to say next may not make sense. Nevertheless, I believe it is the wisest course of action: Consider quality when you think about healthcare planning. A lot of us do not like to spend very much money every month on our health insurance costs. For many people, their health insurance costs throughout their life have been heavily subsidized. Perhaps their employer covered their health insurance costs, or, if they were on some type of individual plan, it could have been subsidized through a government program in some way like the Affordable Care Act.

If you try to keep that mentality of trying to save as much money as possible on your monthly premium and only elect to get Medicare Part B, you might have trouble someday when you start to have real needs when it comes to your healthcare because Part B only covers a portion of medical bills. Getting the best coverage you can might cost you more up front in your monthly premiums. But should that day come when you need a big surgery or have a significant procedure done, you won't be getting a massive bill when you leave the hospital.

You can concentrate on recovering your health, not your financial future.

Think of your health insurance as a way to protect your golden goose. When you are seventy-eight and you start seeing the doctor more regularly and having general healthcare needs or even something scary like a dreaded diagnosis, you don't want to have the goose "taking bullets" left and right, where big chunks are being taken out of it to cover medical bills. Depending on how long you live, that has a great potential to affect how much income you can sustainably draw upon in the latter part of your life. You do not want to be facing the idea of having to try to find work as a bookkeeper or grocery bagger or in phone sales at seventy-eight or eighty-one. To avoid that, it's important to make sure that all your bases are covered.

I realize that these tasks can all start to feel daunting. By the time we think about income planning and investment planning and tax planning, and then we finally get to healthcare planning, I can see folks just throwing their hands up and saying, "What are we doing here? This is just so complicated." It can feel like an endless list of questions. **It is at that point where folks either push into it and end up in a fantastic situation because they have all these variables accounted for, or they just give up and leave their future to circumstance.**

Too often, I have seen that those who do the latter all too often end up leaving very little to their family after dealing with a lot more stress. They end up in a much worse place financially. Maybe they won't run out of money, but they're not maximizing their retirement. They are not getting all the juice out of the orange.

Rather than view these different elements of planning as competing for your attention, view it as a tug-of-war, when properly accounted for, each component is pulling the rope in the same direction with you. With all of the planning elements working in tandem, you can do quite well. If your retirement plan is disjointed, the domino effects can be substantial.

Let's say your healthcare plan is minimal and you have a health need in your late seventies. You are stuck with a bill for 20 percent of a surgical procedure and a hospital stay. That could run into the high five figures or even more. If you must take that money out of your IRA, you don't just have to take out the money for the bill, you have to withdraw enough money to cover the additional taxes on that amount, which may likely push you into a **higher** tax bracket.

It comes back to holistic planning—incorporating the entire picture—and how the plan for each individual is as unique as their fingerprint. It is like a 5,000-piece puzzle. If you don't have each of those different pieces, you're not going to have the whole picture. It is going to be flawed. Don't leave a stray piece hidden in the couch cushions or on the floor.

Timing also plays a significant role in determining the strategy for your healthcare plan. If you are retiring early, let's say before sixty-five, you are most likely going to be looking at individual health insurance. This means shopping for health insurance on the open market in the healthcare marketplace exchange. If you retire before sixty-five and your spouse is still working, you might still be on their employer's plan. That might be a more cost-effective option. If you are someone who has a large pension from a company where you have worked for many years, you may have health insurance as part of your retirement package. This means you could retire early and not be worried about health insurance or staying below certain income thresholds for the purpose of subsidies.

But if that is not your life, if your spouse isn't working, if you don't have eligibility from previous employment, you're almost certainly in a situation where you will be forced to shop for health insurance on the open market.

If you are thinking of retiring at sixty-five, you will immediately go on Medicare. At some point, individual health insurance for those who retire before sixty-five is essentially going to be a bridge until you are eligible for Medicare.

Before I talk about Medicare, though, I think it is important to point out that, similar to tax strategy, we do not want the health insurance tail to wag the retirement dog. When we decide to retire is going to determine what strategy we start to think about for health insurance itself—not the other way around. The number-one reason I see folks not retire early or fail to retire before sixty-five is because of poor health coverage planning. **They believe they only have one option: Simply wait until Medicare becomes available at sixty-five. And they start counting the days.**

That is a false dichotomy. A lot of advisors seem to believe there are basically only two knobs to turn in retirement or financial planning: the first is simply how much you are going to save for retirement? The second is when do you retire?

There is so much more to it than that.

Allow me to offer an example of why timing is pivotal when it comes to healthcare planning. Sam and Beth were between a rock and a hard place. Sam worked for a lumber company for more than twenty years. He had essentially spent his career there. He was moving into retirement at sixty-five. Like most people, he expected to go right on Medicare.

The problem that arose was that his wife was three years younger. Throughout their earnings years, she had her health insurance through his employer plan. When he retired and went on Medicare, she was going to have to go on a COBRA plan—an extension of their current coverage but without the employer's share being paid. Beth was distraught about this because of the costs. COBRA plans are quite expensive, and in her case, it was going to cost $1,100 a month instead of the $250 they were paying for both of them per month. She had the option of shopping on the exchange or taking this COBRA plan.

Because of their income, either option was going to be expensive. How do you make the decision there? It seems like trying to pick the lesser of two evils. "I thought health insurance through the Affordable Care Act was inexpensive," you may say. The truth is, when you shop for individual health insurance through what is commonly called Obamacare, you are eligible for subsidies only if you stay under certain taxable income limits. Sam and Beth were taking out too much in their IRA distributions to qualify for subsidies through the Affordable Care Act.

That situation they faced was an intersection of income planning, tax planning, and healthcare planning. **When you have an intersection of that many obstacles, the potential for the problem to compound goes up significantly.**

A bad income plan and a poor tax strategy with that income plan can have costly consequences. Inefficient tax planning and income planning means you are paying more in taxes than you need to, which means your income is not going as far. It could also result in higher costs for health insurance. Each domino falls one after the other.

Fortunately for Sam and Beth, they were able to catch it before it was too late and adjust their strategy. Instead of paying COBRA at $1,100 a month for Beth's health insurance, they only ended up having to pay about $280 a month for similar coverage after shopping on the exchange for an individual plan. The key was how their plan was designed. Beth was able to qualify for a significant subsidy through the Affordable Care Act because of the way their income was now structured. Instead of taking all that money from a taxable place in their IRA, they were able to lower their taxable income through their first three years of retirement by strategically pulling from a Roth IRA as well as a brokerage account and thus qualify for the subsidy.

Getting an individual health insurance plan is intimidating for most people who have been on their employer's plan throughout their working life. After you have worked at your job for a few months, you go to human resources when you are eligible to receive health insurance through the company, and you might have three options to choose from. The number of options may differ from business to business, but the general concept is the same. You select your option after reviewing the offerings and then you are done.

And then, all of a sudden, you find yourself shopping on the exchange. I do not believe people should be intimidated when shopping for health insurance on the open market. It is just like buying insurance for your car or for your house. You go to an insurance agent, pick out what is best for you, and move on. You might not have made those types of choices before, but it is not something that should intimidate you if you're working with an experienced professional who understands your situation and is sharp at what they do. The key is working with the right professional who will act as a guide, not as a salesperson.

WHO UNDERSTANDS MEDICARE?

I have already mentioned Medicare, but I would like to discuss this government healthcare coverage in a little more detail. Medicare has multiple alphabet components: Parts A, B, and D, along with Medicare Advantage and Medicare supplements.

- **PART A** is your hospital insurance and it is free. Everyone must file for this when they turn sixty-five, even if they are still working. For those who are still working—and that age will grow as the retirement age for full Social Security climbs—Medicare often serves as a secondary coverage to your employer's health insurance plan.

- **PART B** covers 80 percent of your medical expenses, and it is not free. There is a monthly premium, though it is not nearly as expensive as COBRA.

- **PART D** is commonly referred to as prescription drug coverage, and its cost varies depending on the prescription drugs you need and plan you pick. Bear in mind that even with Part B, you are responsible for 20 percent of your medical costs, which can still amount to a substantial sum depending on the care you need.

The rates for Medicare vary from year to year and are dependent, in part, on your income. This is another intersection of income planning and tax planning with healthcare coverage in mind. Then we get into the Medicare Advantage plans—sometimes called Part C.

- **MEDICARE ADVANTAGE** plans are offered by certain approved private insurance companies. In most cases, you need to use certain healthcare providers that participate in a certain plan network, but this is at least an available option and often less costly than regular Medicare.

Medicare Supplement goes beyond what I have just mentioned.

- **"MED SUP"** is often referred to as Medigap, because it fits into the coverage gaps of Medicare Parts A, B, and D. I tend to steer folks more toward a Medigap option than a Medicare Advantage option. But as I have said many times, each individual's situation is unique and should be treated accordingly.

I realize this can all seem like alphabet soup. When we are talking about Medicare, it is intimidating. At the end of the day, it be hard to understand not only because of all the letters but also because it's always changing, and even for us professionals, it can be challenging to keep up with the changes.

Bear in mind that if you are age fifty right now, it is likely that Medicare is going to look different by the time you get to sixty-five. It is hard to plan for it now because of the uncertainty. We can account for a certain amount of dollars set aside for the cost of health insurance, but until you are nearly there, it is hard to know exactly what you should be filing for.

I cannot stress enough the importance of healthcare planning. It is a significant piece of risk mitigation. Even the 20 percent of a medical cost not covered by Medicare can run into the high five figures or more, and a lump sum cost like that can be a very risky cost for your retirement. Just looking at Parts B and D alone might not be enough. In my opinion, you would be well served to consider not just A and B and D, but also Medigap coverage or other options that can supplement what Medicare does not cover.

LONG-TERM CARE INSURANCE

Costs are rising for long-term care and those can be difficult to handle if you must pull from your assets. You do not want to kill the golden goose later in its life because that will very much put you on rocky ground financially.

In some cultures, as you age, you just stay with your family and they take care of you. But more and more in the United States, we see people who say, "I don't want to be a burden to my kids." We've all heard about the sandwich generation—the middle-aged sons and daughters who are raising their kids and taking care of their aging parents. The people in that situation are in a tough spot because it is pulling on their time as well as their wallet. They are in "the messy middle" of life when they have young kids going through school and there are all kinds of expenses. They have real difficulty trying to reach financial freedom themselves because of the cost of raising a family, putting kids through college, and tending to aging parents, never mind how difficult it is for them to save for their own retirement.

Consider another factor beyond the financial implications as well: The sandwiched middle generation may not have the ability to provide the kind of care that Mom and Dad need if Mom and Dad don't have the money to care for themselves. I'm talking about in-home caregivers (not family members), retirement home living, rehab facilities, assisted living, and nursing home and memory care.

In order for you and your family to be prepared for long-term care needs, the most common solution is to simply purchase a long-term care policy from an insurance provider. I see this type of solution often work best particularly if you are doing this when you are younger and not close to retirement. You can get much better rates on a long-term care policy when you are younger, say forties and fifties.

These policies are generally prohibitively expensive when you start to look at them in your sixties, at which point you may ask yourself, "Why would I fork out this much money and there's no certainty that I would actually need long-term care insurance?" In other words, you may or may not actually use the coverage. Are you just going to throw a significant amount of money away every month? Of course, the trade-off is you might genuinely need it one day. Do you risk not having it at all and then being hit with the high cost of long-term care?

In my view, long-term care insurance is like the disability insurance that you have during your working years. Many employers offer insurance for short-term or long-term disability, with the premium coming out of your paycheck each pay period. The likelihood of someone needing that insurance over the course of their working life is quite low in most professions. But it is more and more likely that people are going to have a long-term care need because they are living longer and fewer people are relying on family to care for them as they age. Therefore, having that protection is critical.

Think of the story of the three little pigs. When the wolf comes knocking on your door, do you have a house of straw? Do you have a house of sticks? Or do you have a house of bricks? If you do not account for the potential cost of long-term care, it just comes back to the risk of something happening later in your retirement that costs you a ton of money, depletes your assets entirely, and leaves you destitute.

Alternatively, you could look at life insurance with a long-term care rider. You want to be careful with this because not all these options are created equal. Make sure you understand the benefit that comes with the policy. It can be a much more cost-effective strategy, but make sure you understand the benefit that comes with the policy.

Typically with these types of specialty insurance policies, you have a normal life insurance policy where you pay a premium. At the end of your life, you have a death benefit that goes to your family. But you also have a long-term care rider attached that allows you, under certain circumstances, to use the death benefit to pay for long-term care. It is like an advance on the benefit.

To be fair, the cost is going to be like a normal long-term care policy, but at least there is a guarantee of somebody getting a benefit: Either you will presumably use it for long-term care or your beneficiaries are going to get a lump sum payout when you die. With this option, at least you know you are paying for something.

Those are the two primary ways you could get long-term care insurance. Don't hesitate to shop around for that coverage. Terms and rates have changed significantly since long-term care insurance first entered the marketplace and figure to continue to evolve as we move forward and the bulk of the baby boom generation reaches its twilight years. But there is a third option available: self-insurance.

SELF-INSURANCE

Many people have begun going this route rather than buying an expensive long-term care insurance policy. They get Medicare Parts A, B, and D and then start setting money aside every month, earmarking it for long-term care needs in the future. It can be nice to do this if you are starting long-term care planning later, such as in your mid-sixties, presuming you have enough savings.

> **"By taking this step, you have put yourself in the driver's seat and you have more control over your funds."**

Perhaps you are able to retire comfortably and you have some leftover room in your budget. Instead of spending that $1,000 a month on a long-term care policy for you and your spouse as you approach your retirement, you put money in a Health Savings Account during your working years (which I'll explain a little further on).

You could even earmark some of your savings—perhaps $50,000 to $100,000—invest it, and let that balance grow over time. You are most likely to use a long-term care benefit when you are older, in your late seventies or eighties. By taking this step, you have put yourself in the driver's seat and you have more control over your funds.

There is a down side to self-insurance. It is riskier, because it is dependent on your ability to pay the bills if the worst-case scenario does happen. You assume all the financial risks there. That is why you really want to weigh everything to see what is best for you. For certain people, it can be a good option, particularly if you are planning at or close to retirement and you have some savings built up. History shows long-term care is typically needed for about two years or less. Either you have recovered enough to leave the healthcare facility or you are no longer with us.

Even as you are weighing how to handle your long-term care or healthcare costs, you can't forget about tax efficiency. There are a couple of ways to achieve that: a Roth IRA, a Health Savings Account, or an HSA. An HSA is a fantastic account because it offers a triple tax advantage. Contributions go in pretax, savings grows tax-free, and money gets pulled out tax-free if it is used for qualified health expenses. Many companies offer those, so make use of that if it is available. You can only contribute to an HSA after you retire if you are not yet enrolled in Medicare, so make sure to start early with an HSA if you can.

Roth IRAs can be another way to ease the tax burden of a substantial medical bill. Remember: Since a Roth IRA is funded with after-tax dollars, withdrawing from your Roth is tax-free and you can draw funds from there without throwing off your entire tax picture. One way to think about it is as a rainy day fund or an emergency fund. It is not a perfect solution, but it is an option with some flexibility.

You may decide to earmark $50,000 to $100,000 of your savings in your Roth IRA and just let it grow. You could even take an aggressive posture on your investing in that Roth since you may well have ten to fifteen years or longer before you might need it for long-term care. By that time, it can grow into a substantial sum.

In an ideal world, I would recommend a blend of the two long-term healthcare strategies: a good insurance policy as well as some self-insurance so you have some flexibility built in.

PILLAR 4 SUMMARY:

1. Mitigating Risk: Healthcare planning is crucial to avoid depleting retirement savings on unexpected medical expenses. It's about protecting your "golden goose."

2. Healthcare Costs: Medicare Parts A, B, D, Advantage, and Supplement plans each offer different coverage options. Choose wisely to avoid large out-of-pocket expenses.

3. Long-Term Care Options: Consider long-term care insurance, life insurance with a long-term care rider, or self-insuring to prepare for potential future needs.

4. Tax Efficiency: Use Health Savings Accounts (HSAs) and Roth IRAs to manage healthcare costs tax-efficiently.

ACTION STEPS:

- **Evaluate your healthcare coverage options early.**

- **Plan for potential long-term care needs.**

- **Maximize tax-efficient accounts like HSAs and Roth IRAs.**

PILLAR 5

"YOUR LEGACY ON THIS PLANET, WHEN YOU LEAVE, IS HOW MANY HEARTS YOU TOUCHED."

— *PATTI DAVIS* —

LEGACY PLANNING

WHO GETS YOUR ASSETS, WHAT DO THEY GET, AND WHEN?

What kind of legacy would you like to leave for your loved ones, for your community, perhaps even for the world?

This is an important piece of retirement planning that many of us don't often think about as soon or as much as we should. No matter what you want your legacy to look like, it is vital to ensure that your hard-earned assets go to those you love, to your beneficiaries, in the most tax-efficient manner possible. At Bright Lake, we work with estate attorneys to make sure assets are structured properly not only to align with our clients' goals but also from a tax standpoint.

In some ways, your legacy planning is the culmination of the pillars of planning I've discussed coming together. I mentioned this sort of overlap before in the previous chapter as I discussed healthcare planning. For this reason, I like to view the fourth and fifth pillars—healthcare planning and legacy planning—as aspects of advanced planning.

When we think about legacy planning, a couple thoughts come to my mind right away. One is a client who came into my office and said, "Ted, I want my last check to bounce." What he was referring to was that he did not want to leave a dime behind. He wanted to enjoy all his savings and go out with a zero balance. It makes me laugh, because it is funny. But we do not want to fly that close to the sun—unless, of course, you know the exact day you are going to die.

For some people, legacy planning is important, and they have certain monetary goals. For others, legacy is defined in ways beyond how much money they will pass on to family and loved ones. It may be in the memories they make with their family while they are living or checking off items on their bucket list—the national parks, the cruise, the vacation home, the last grandchild through college, a special wedding, a fiftieth anniversary party, a gift to your alma mater, a lasting contribution to your church or favorite charity, or even finally beating everyone at bridge.

Whatever you want your legacy to look like, it is important to plan for it so that it can happen. Otherwise, you may take too much risk and run out of money, or not get around to doing everything you wanted to do.

PASSING OFF WHAT YOU EARNED

Regardless of their plan, I urge my clients to avoid probate. That is what happens when someone dies without a trust that spells out how you want your assets distributed. A revocable living trust does not have to be complicated. Structuring your trust and assets correctly is important because it means you get money back in your pocket and more of it eventually goes where you want it to rather than to Uncle Sam or a team of expensive lawyers arguing with a judge who decides where your assets go. As they say, if you think that setting up a trust is expensive, wait until they hand you the bill for not having one!

> **PROBATE:**
>
> **Probate is the legal process of settling a deceased person's estate, which includes validating the will, paying off debts, and distributing their assets to heirs.**

We've all heard that **it is not about how much you make, it is about how much you keep.** Usually, we think about that as referring to taxes. Probate is sort of Uncle Sam's last chance to get into your pocket, to reach in and take those golden eggs away from you in the form of estate taxes. Basically, a strong estate plan is an extension of protecting your golden goose for future generations. We have to protect the goose for whoever is going to receive it once you pass.

Especially as your net worth increases, having proper estate plans and tax plans for your estate is just extremely important. Otherwise, your heirs are going to get absolutely waxed by taxes? When it comes to your passing, you have already paid tax on this money, presumably. If we are not careful with a plan, your money could be double taxed.

My point being, legacy planning is another aspect of holistic retirement planning. It is all connected. If you do all this planning up to this point, and then you stop and do not have any legacy plan, you're going to be in a difficult place—or, at least, your family will be. You have worked so hard, you may as well make the final effort to make sure that things get passed on in a way that aligns with your goals. Your legacy should have your fingerprints all over it.

Did you know that, by the year 2045, $72 trillion is going to pass on to different heirs? Beneficiaries will receive that money as the baby boomer generation leaves us. Almost $12 trillion more is going to be donated to charities. With so much money involved, you can see why effective planning is important.

How do we devise an effective plan? Let's think about the three W's: who, what, and when. Who gets the money? What are they going to get? When are they going to get it?

Who gets the money should be obvious. If "John and Mary" pass away, who might get the money? Their children, of course. If they have three kids, they might split that up in some way—probably equally.

What are the children receiving? They are receiving assets. It might be cash, it might be stocks or bonds, it might be property that could include vehicles or the family home. Naturally, John and Mary may designate specific heirlooms or mementos to certain children.

> **THE 3 W's:**
>
> **Who gets your money?**
>
> **What are they going to get?**
>
> **When are they going to get it?**

Finally, **when** are they going to get it? Often, as you would imagine, that will likely occur when John and Mary pass away. However, there are all kinds of options with the question of when. Many families we have planned with over the years have opted to advance a portion of what they would otherwise leave as an inheritance ahead of time so they can help their kids with a down payment on a home and help with the education of their grandchildren, and certainly to enjoy making memories with their family. Other circumstances require disbursements under certain conditions over the course of time. Ultimately, the assets should be a blessing, not a curse.

WRITING A POWERFUL ESTATE PLAN

Have you ever played with LEGO, either as a child or with your children and grandchildren? Sometimes, the LEGO instructions are simple. Sometimes, they are incredibly complex. When I was a kid, I built a LEGO Star Wars Millennium Falcon with my dad. It was super complicated. It took us several weeks to build the whole ship, but it was a memorable time. My point is, whether what you are doing is relatively simple or far more complex, you need proper instructions. When you think about it, you are leaving instructions for your family, your loved ones, for when you are no longer with them. You want those instructions to be as clear as possible.

The next step is very practical. You must prepare and finalize your documentation. Think of your plan as framing a new home. When you finalize your documents, you are putting up walls. A lot of thought must go into the documentation for your legacy plan, and to properly, do that you are going to need to hire an estate attorney.

At our office, we believe this is such an important part of planning that we keep an estate attorney on retainer. Of course, many of our clients already have a trust in place, so we are always collaborating with new attorneys as well. Once we have the three W's—who, what, and when—sorted out, we are going to have to put the actual plan together. It might be a trust, it might be a will, it might be a durable power of attorney and healthcare directives. In most cases, it is a combination of all those documents that convey your final wishes.

One common tool many people use is a revocable living trust. Most people will also have a will of some kind, even if it is just a pour-over will. A pour-over will is a last will and testament that captures any assets that are not included in or transferred to a living trust. Think of it as a safety net.

From there, you have durable power of attorney and healthcare directives to consider. A healthcare directive is a combination of a living will (and designates a healthcare surrogate) and a durable power of attorney. It gives direction on medication and resuscitation and various treatment questions that doctors could have if you are ill or injured and otherwise unable to make healthcare decisions for yourself. The durable power of attorney is someone assigned to make financial decisions on your behalf if you are unable to or are too sick to do it yourself.

The bottom line, though—and I would say the biggest bullet we are dodging—is probate. I mentioned before it is expensive. It is also a difficult process to go through, and you do not want to subject your family to that. What happens in probate if you don't have a will or an estate plan in place is that your money and your assets that you have worked very hard to build up are taken and placed into the hands of a judge who has all of the control. This is someone who does not know you or your family. On top of that, they have very strict legal ramifications within which they must operate. The results can be devastating to your estate.

I do not want to belabor this point too much, but if shedding light on the potential consequences happens to be the kick-in-the-pants someone reading this needs to get off the couch and do the necessary planning, then it is worth it. **Let me tell you: Those who have had to go through probate will not be hesitating to set up a will or a trust so their loved ones do not have to endure it as well.** The bottom line is when we prepare and finalize the documents, we avoid that problem.

Putting a trust or will in place is not **holistic** estate tax planning in and of itself. What it does, however, is give you legal protection. One of those safeguards, as I have highlighted, is the avoidance of probate. Further, you gain liability protection of the assets for the family. Just like your investment plan and your will, however, you should not just set it and forget it. It is wise to periodically review your estate documents as your circumstances change so they best reflect your needs and wishes and family composition.

Once you have a will or trust (or both) in place, you can focus on estate tax planning. You have heard me say, **"It's not about how much you make, it's about how much you keep."** That is significant not just in reference to your taxes, but also to legacy planning as well. Once we have the baseline structure in place, we can take advantage of estate tax opportunities.

ADDING STRATEGY TO YOUR ESTATE PLAN

When it comes to specifics, of course, what could work very well for one person may make zero sense for another. This is where input and guidance from a trusted financial planner can be so significant. You want to think about the factors at play, from a tax standpoint, when you pass away.

I will mention a couple of strategies to consider when putting together your legacy plan, though more detailed plans should be put together following consultation with a financial advisor who concentrates in retirement planning as well as with an estate planning attorney.

I have addressed IRAs previously in this book. Some trusts are designed to hold IRAs and some are not. Typically, you want an individual to be the beneficiary of an IRA because it is much less complicated. But regardless of how your trust is structured, if you have a traditional IRA or a traditional 401(k) that is being inherited, it is still fully taxable to beneficiaries at your death. When you think about the rest of the tax burden that also may be flowing to them, they may get double hammered or triple tagged because they may be pushed into a much higher tax bracket as they also have their own income to consider. You probably will not want them to run into that, so you may consider paying some of the taxes early on traditional IRAs by converting or transferring them to a Roth IRA. The taxes are paid at that time, and since taxes on Roth IRAs have already been paid, your beneficiaries would be spared that burden.

> **STEPPED-UP TAX BASIS:**
> The value of an inherited asset is set to its worth when the previous owner passed away, which can lower your taxes when you sell it.

For assets that have appreciated substantially, it is wise to look at the consequences of what is called a **stepped-up tax basis**. What is that? Let's look at an example. Harold bought a house and property for $50,000 when he was thirty years old. A half-century later, it is worth $500,000. Let us assume it is not his primary residence. If Harold sells that home before he passes away, he pays long-term capital gains on $450,000 because of the increase in value over those fifty years.

But if he holds on to that property and allows it to be inherited by his children after he passes away, they are going to have what is called a stepped-up tax basis. That means they inherited a property with a principal value of $500,000. They could sell that home immediately and not have any tax burden on it for the increase in value.

One of my clients was an executive at a large energy company, and he had a lot of stock options with the company that he accumulated over the years. He held onto those stock purchases his entire career and they increased substantially in value. If he would have sold the stock before he passed away, he would have had a huge capital gain tax. But he held onto them. The stocks were inherited by his children and split up equally. They received stock certificates that went into an investment account for them. If they wanted to sell the stock at some point, they could at a stepped-up tax basis, meaning they would not have the capital gains consequence their father would have if he had been the one who sold.

These are just a couple of the strategies to consider when exploring your legacy planning.

For those with substantial estates well into the eight figures, there are other considerations to make. There are federal and state consequences to estate taxes, and changes are coming. The Tax Cuts and Jobs Act passed in 2017 doubled the federal estate tax limit to what is currently at the time of this writing $12.92 million. What that means is if you die next year and your estate is less than $12.92 million, you will not owe any federal estate taxes. Only the amount above that $12.92 million would be subject to federal estate tax, which is tiered but quickly reaches 40 percent. That figure is per person, not per family.

When the Tax Cuts and Jobs Act phases out after 2025, the limit drops to $5 million plus inflation adjustments—or essentially what it was before the bill passed. With that reduction looming, people with substantial estates may want to consider strategic gifting ahead of time. In 2023, the gifting limit before you must report anything to the IRS is $17,000 per recipient per year.

Now let's look at estate taxes on the state level. The estate tax limits vary from state to state. California, for example, has no estate tax limits. Oregon, meanwhile, has an estate tax limit of $1 million. Anything above that figure is taxed.

What you need to know as you begin your estate tax planning is whether your state has an estate tax and what the current rate is. In a state such as Oregon, between the value of your home and any other property, along with your retirement account, it can be very easy to reach that $1 million threshold and thus increase the tax burden for your heirs.

Therefore, we need strategies to minimize estate taxes, so more of what you have accumulated is passed on to your loved ones. One direct way to minimize taxes is through strategic gifting. Remember the gifting limit of $17,000 that I mentioned? That is per person, so a husband and wife could each gift $17,000 to each of their children each year. What is less commonly understood is that you can give more than that $17,000 limit. You simply must properly report it on your taxes. This strategy, when implemented properly, can be extremely powerful.

I've seen high–net worth families implement strategic gifting and estate planning strategies that ended up saving their heirs nearly seven figures in so-called death taxes. By strategically gifting specific assets with the right strategy, you may lower the value of your estate, making less of your accumulated assets subject to estate taxes.

Others like to designate charities to receive portions of their estate upon their passing. You could even donate to a charity while you are still alive and receive a tax write-off. That would be another way to reduce the taxable value of your estate.

ESTATE PLANNING IS MORE THAN MONETARY

Many families we work with view legacy as something much beyond financial matters alone. Some even set up a family foundation, where family members choose charities to support. I am thinking about a couple who started a small business building components for appliances. The business grew dramatically, and they became quite wealthy. They raised several children and instilled core family values of generosity and giving back to the community.

They set up a family foundation, and once a year, the whole family gets together over a long weekend to enjoy each other's company and discuss the gifts the family foundation will dispense in the coming year. But it goes beyond writing a check. They volunteer at organizations such as the Boys & Girls Club or at church events. They do not just give money; they offer their hands and feet to help those in need—and the entire family is involved. That is creating a culture in their family. In my mind, that is huge. **Their legacy is more than financial.**

My grandparents were a lot like this. We were taught to give not just of our treasure, but of our time and talent as well. This ties in well with another aspect of legacy planning: leaving more than money. The irony is, for most people, "inheritance" is thought of as strictly financial. But when others think of the word legacy, they think of family traditions—recipes, core values, regular gatherings, memories passed on from one generation to the next.

It is important to have those conversations with your family ahead of time. I hear more and more people are doing oral histories and video recordings to save memories and traditions and cherished stories. It is a way to document pieces of family history. If you want to leave a legacy of a culture in your family, it must be an intentional effort.

It is also important to have "the talk"—no, not about the birds and the bees. The one about who is going to be the executor of the estate. What are the expectations being set for the other members in the family? What should they expect? Who will receive which family heirlooms? I have seen this happen in my own family.

When my grandfather passed away, there was a discussion—thankfully, argument is certainly too strong of a word—about who would get to keep his Bible. He was a devout man and his Bible is a family treasure. Though it might be an afterthought, who will keep Mom's wedding ring can be an important and emotional conversation to have. It is best to sort out as much of that ahead of time as you reasonably can so there are not unpleasant surprises or painful conflicts later.

Remember, everything does not have to be precisely the same for everyone. It should be whatever works best for all involved. I am reminded of a client, Janice. She has two daughters. One of them is much better with money than the other. She is simply more responsible. Janice set up her estate so that this daughter receives a full lump sum of an inheritance. To keep this simple, I'll say that her second daughter is not in a great situation. Because of that, Janice set up a trust that will provide her a certain amount every year and every month, depending on the situation. They are ultimately getting the same amount of money—just in different ways.

These can be difficult conversations, but they need to happen. Emotions can run high, so consider even having a trusted third party or advisor involved to help explain how things will be handled.

PILLAR 5 SUMMARY:

1. Legacy Goals: Consider what legacy you want to leave for your loved ones, community, or charities. Plan to ensure your assets are distributed according to your wishes in the most tax-efficient way.

2. Avoid Probate: A revocable living trust prevents your estate from going through probate, which can be costly and time-consuming. Proper estate planning protects your assets for future generations.

3. Estate Planning Documents: Essential documents include a will, revocable living trust, durable power of attorney, and healthcare directives. Review these periodically to reflect changes in your circumstances.

4. Tax Efficiency: Use strategies like Roth IRA conversions and gifting to reduce tax burdens on your heirs.

ACTION STEPS:

- **Establish a trust or will.**

- **Work with estate attorneys to optimize tax strategies.**

- **Discuss your legacy plans with your family.**

PART THREE

CONCLUSION

"THERE IS A WHOLE
NEW KIND OF LIFE
AHEAD, FULL OF
EXPERIENCES JUST
WAITING TO HAPPEN.
SOME CALL IT
RETIREMENT.
I CALL IT BLISS."

— BETTY SULLIVAN —

YOUR FINANCIAL HOUSE

WELCOME HOME

As I bring this book to a close, I want to share a few thoughts. Thank you for taking this journey with me. Retirement is not just the finish line at the end of your marathon of working years, where you are running endlessly in the rat race until—boom!—you collapse into your recliner in front of the TV when you reach the retirement tape.

Certainly, your working years are a large arc in the story line of your life. **But retirement is not the end.** You are not just retiring from, you are retiring to, a life after work. That is why I stress the value of planning and preparation.

I like to use a unique math problem here: 1+1 = 4.

Now, everyone knows that is not basic math. It is not even "new math." What that equation represents is that the value of planning compounds over time.

When we have all five of the pillars I have mentioned in building our financial house, that is a tremendous accomplishment. In its completion, it allows everything about your financial life to be efficient. We don't just have the value of having an income plan, or an investment plan, or a tax plan, or a healthcare plan, or a legacy plan. We have them all together and they dovetail with each other and it all fits like a glove.

I am a numbers guy. I recognize that one plus one does not equal four. But I also recognize that compounding an exponential value is one of a mathematician's Eight Wonders of the World. What we have found to be true, working with retirees every single day, is that when we layer on all these different aspects of planning together, their retirements are maximized. Our clients go from maybe having a good situation to having an exceptional situation.

A lot of advisors only focus on one or two of those pillars. **When you have a holistic plan that covers all five of the different pillars, the value compounds.**

The five-pillar process we walk through is called the Launch Your Retirement™ Blueprint. It is a step-by-step process for building a holistic plan for your retirement. It allows us to look at your family's unique situation, and all the various pieces of your puzzle, and allows us to pull them together. We then mathematically test your assets to determine what money strategies are going to be the best fit for you.

When I sit down with prospective clients, as much as I believe they should be evaluating me as their potential financial advisor, I think it is important for me to evaluate the clients with whom I want to work. That is why I typically ask myself two questions when I sit down and meet with folks:

- **FIRST**, do I believe that I can make a significant impact on your financial life? I ask this first question because I want to know from a technical and analytical standpoint that we'll be able to make measurable improvements to your financial life.
- **SECOND**, do I believe we would be a good fit?

I want to make sure that we are a good fit because we need to make sure we can build a foundation of trust in order to have a long-term relationship. This is vital because with any long-term relationship, there are going to be points where you must come together and collaborate.

Also, when I come to work every day, I want to be excited about the meetings that I have on my calendar because we won't just be sitting down with our clients when we're putting a plan together. We will be with them over the next five, ten, or twenty years or more, and likely guiding their whole family through what will reasonably be a very difficult time—when their loved one has passed on and left a legacy.

I do think that, when you are talking with an advisor—no matter who it is, you should ask yourself those two questions as well.

You want to have confidence in your plan, and you want to have confidence in your advisor. Practically speaking, there are inevitable ebbs and flows in your own personal life and emotional life as you navigate the season of life that is retirement. But when it comes to the financial markets, nothing happens in a straight line. There will be rocky moments as well as great wins as far as growth in the markets. **Making sure you have a foundation of trust in order to navigate those ups and downs is important.**

> Knowing where to start and knowing what questions to ask is half the battle.

At Bright Lake, we help hardworking Americans realize the retirement they have always dreamed of. You may wonder why I chose to write this book. I want to make information about money and retirement available to everyone—whether they are our clients or not. Some advisors want to keep everything behind the locked door or hidden away in some safe somewhere, and once you hire them, they will take care of everything. That is just not how I work; I want you to see what we are doing. If you like how we do it, then great, we would be happy to help.

But at the end of the day, people need retirement information, whether you're just starting out or coming to the end of your career. Whether you decide to work with us or not, that is not the point. It is my belief that you need to have the information. Knowing where to start and knowing what questions to ask is half the battle.

If you are reading this book, you can take this framework and go out and say, "You know what, I'm going to build my own thing." That is a risk I leave on the table when I put this information out there. I have come to terms with that because, at the end of the day, my goal is to help as many people as possible live their dream retirement.

Your retirement, just like the plan you have put together for it, should be as unique as your fingerprint. Your transition from a life of working to a life in retirement, going from saver to spender, is the greatest transition you will ever make in your financial life.

Whether you have $50,000, $500,000, or $5 million, it is important to make sure you have accounted for these five pillars of planning. How you build your financial house is going to play a significant role in what your retirement ends up looking like, how much you leave to your kids, how much of your retirement you can enjoy, how maximized your situation is going to be. In order to make this huge transition, you need to make sure that you have everything properly accounted for so that you can end up focusing on what really matters.

You will recall the story about my grandparents at the beginning of this book. That night at the restaurant was the inspiration point for everything that I do. Here is what happened next: My grandparents left that dinner, where we were all sitting around the table under an umbrella of awkwardness, and they realized that was not how they wanted their retirement to go, just ordering the cheap chicken dinner.

So they decided to take steps and make a change to put a plan in place—not only for their own peace of mind but also so that, the next time we were all sitting around a dinner table, celebrating a birthday, an anniversary, or some happy event, the only worry was about making sure that whomever was supposed to be celebrated that day felt celebrated and loved.

The truth is my grandparents, along with the rest of my family, did not want to have a Scrooge mentality of, "We'll retire, but we'll just rub pennies together along the way." That was never who they were, so it was not going to work for them that way. They just needed to make sure that they had a plan in place so they could live their perfect days in retirement the way they wished.

You deserve a great retirement. You deserve a great retirement where you don't have to worry about how you're going to pay the monthly bills. You deserve a great retirement where you get to hear your grandkids come up to you and say, "Thank you, Grandpa. Thank you, Grandma, for taking us out to dinner tonight." You deserve a retirement where, if you want to travel, you can travel. If you want to spend time with your grandkids, you can spend time with your grandkids. And if you want to serve, you can serve.

You deserve

a great

retirement!

TERMS

401(k) account: a retirement savings plan offered by many American employers that has tax advantages for the saver and is named after a section of the US Internal Revenue Code that created the plan

403(b) account: a retirement account for employees of public schools and other tax-exempt organizations, similar to a 401(k)

Annuities: contracts issued and distributed or sold by financial institutions where the funds are invested, often with the goal of paying out a fixed income stream later

Asset allocation: This is an investment strategy that attempts to balance risk versus reward by adjusting the percentage of each asset in an investment portfolio according to the investor's risk tolerance, goals, and investment time frame

Asset location: a tax-minimization investment strategy that takes advantage of different types of investment accounts having differing tax treatments and organizes the asset allocation accordingly

Basis point: One hundredth of 1 percent (0.01 percent), used primarily in expressing differences of interest rates

Brokerage account: an investment account that allows you to buy and sell a variety of investments, such as stocks, bonds, mutual funds, and exchange-traded funds (ETFs)

CEO: chief executive officer, the highest-ranking executive in a company

CFO: chief financial officer, the senior executive responsible for the financial affairs of a business or other institution

COBRA: Consolidated Omnibus Budget Reconciliation Act of 1985 gives individuals who experience a job loss or other qualifying event (such as retirement) the option of continuing their current health insurance coverage for a limited amount of time

Ethics: moral principles that govern a person's behavior or the conducting of an activity

Diversification: a strategy that mixes a wide variety of investments within a portfolio to limit exposure to any single asset or risk

Donor-advised fund: a charitable giving vehicle administered by a public charity created to manage charitable donations on behalf of organizations, families, or individuals (To participate in a donor-advised fund, a donating individual or organization opens an account in the fund and deposits cash, securities, or other financial instruments. They surrender ownership of anything they put in the fund, but retain advisory privileges over how their account is invested and how it distributes money to charities.)

Dot-com: a business that conducts business primarily through a website

Durable power of attorney: a legal document that authorizes someone else to handle matters such as finances or healthcare decisions on your behalf if you are not able to

ETF: exchange-traded funds, a type of pooled investment security that operates much like a mutual fund

Fiduciary: an individual or organization that has a legal duty to act in the best interest of someone else

Holistic financial planning: a strategy designed to help you create a plan that covers the individual parts of your financial life while ensuring that they all work together

Inflation: a general increase in prices and fall in the purchasing value of money

Investment management: the professional asset management of various securities, including shareholdings, bonds, and other assets, such as real estate, to meet specified investment goals

IRA: individual retirement account, a long-term savings account that people with earned income can use to save for the future while enjoying certain tax advantages (IRAs are designed primarily for self-employed people who do not have access to workplace retirement accounts such as a 401(k). Contributions to an

IRA are tax deductible, but withdrawals are taxed as income and there are penalties for early withdrawals.)

Laddered income strategy: an approach based on allocating portions of your total investment at different times, rather than investing everything all at once, which creates staggered maturity dates, allowing your returns to mature in regular intervals

Legacy: an amount of money or property left to someone in a will

Living will: a legal document (also called a healthcare directive) that specifies the type of medical care an individual does or does not want in the event they are unable to communicate their wishes

Long-term care rider: a living benefit on a life insurance policy that lets you access a portion of the policy's death benefit every month to pay for long-term care expenses

Managed fund: a pool of money spread across a range of assets such as company shares, government bonds, or property

Medicare: a federal system of health insurance for people over sixty-five years of age and certain younger people with disabilities

Municipal bond: a bond issued by state or local governments or entities they establish such as authorities and special districts; interest income from these bonds is often exempt from state and federal taxation

Mutual funds: a professionally managed investment fund that pools money from many investors to purchase securities

Non-qualified account: an account into which after-tax money is deposited, so only the interest earned is taxable

Pay it forward: respond to a person's kindness to oneself by being kind to someone else

Platform fee: a fee charged for conducting investment transactions online; the amount can vary depending on the platform used

Portfolio: a range of investments held by a person or organization

Pour-over will: a document wherein the writer of a will creates a trust and decrees in the will that the property in their estate shall, at the time of their death, be distributed to the trustee of the trust for disposition

Private equity firm: investment partnership that buys and manages companies or assets before selling them

Probate: the legal process that your estate goes through after you die (It is always more straightforward if you have a will or trust that expresses your wishes clearly. If a person dies without a will, the court in the state of residence will determine who inherits the decedent's possessions.)

Prospectus: a formal document required by and filed with the Securities and Exchange Commission (SEC) that provides details about an investment offering to the public; a prospectus is filed for offerings of stocks, bonds, and mutual funds

Qualified account: an account in which you can deposit money without paying taxes on it until it is withdrawn

Qualified charitable distribution: a distribution from your individual retirement account (IRA) to a qualified charity (You must be age seventy and a half or older to make a qualified charitable distribution. A QCD is not taxed and is not included in your taxable income.)

Required minimum distribution (RMD): the amount of money that must be withdrawn from an employer-sponsored retirement plan to avoid tax consequences (The age at which RMDs must begin is seventy-three. If you have multiple accounts, you will typically need to calculate the RMD for each and may need to take distributions from each of them.)

Revocable living trust: an estate planning tool you can use to determine who will get your property when you die ("Revocable" means you can change your trust as your circumstances or wishes change. "Living" means you make those changes during your lifetime.)

Risk tolerance: the degree of risk that an investor is willing to endure given the volatility in the value of an investment; risk tolerance often determines the type and number of investments that an individual chooses

Roth IRA: similar to a traditional IRA but funded with after-tax dollars, meaning contributions are not tax deductible and withdrawals are tax-free

Sales load: a load is a fee that the fund charges in order to compensate the professional or institution that sells you shares of the mutual fund; the fee can be charged when you buy the shares (front-end load) or when you sell them (back-end load)

Sandwich generation: those who are caring for young children and aging parents simultaneously

Social Security: a government program designed to provide retirement support for American workers who pay into the system during their working years

Stepped-up tax basis: a tax policy that looks at the market value of assets at the time a person inherits them instead of the value when the prior owner purchased the assets

Survivorship: the legal right assigned to a survivor of people with a joint interest to take the whole on the death of the others; often seen in action when one person in a marriage dies and jointly owned property is passed to the surviving spouse

Tax loss harvesting: a strategy investors can use to reduce the total amount of capital gains taxes due from the sale of profitable investments (The strategy involves selling an asset or security at a net loss, then using the proceeds to purchase a similar asset or security, maintaining the portfolio's overall balance.)

ACKNOWLEDGMENTS

I would like to express my deepest gratitude to the individuals who have played a crucial role in the completion of this book. Their support, guidance, and inspiration have been invaluable, and I am truly indebted to them.

First and foremost, I would like to extend my heartfelt appreciation to our wonderful clients, the Bright Lake Wealth Management Family. Your trust in the expertise of our team and organization is humbling. Your feedback and experiences have been instrumental in providing practical insights and real-world examples that will undoubtedly benefit future retirees. I hope you have learned as much from us as we have from you—from schoolteachers to business owners, from CPAs and CFOs to fathers and mothers. We are so grateful to serve you.

To my beloved wife, Kassie, I am forever grateful for your unwavering support and understanding. The resilience you've shown and the patient sacrifices you have made behind the scenes for our family leave me in awe. Thank you for your encouragement and belief in my vision.

To my children, Ethan, Olivia, and Lincoln, you are my greatest inspiration. Your boundless energy, love, and curiosity remind me every day why I strive to be the best version of myself. Thank you for your understanding and encouragement and for reminding me of the importance of balance in life. Your presence and love remind me of the importance of planning for the future and the significance of the work we do in helping others achieve their retirement dreams.

My parents, who have been my pillars of support from the beginning. Your unconditional love, guidance, and belief in my abilities have shaped the person I am today. Your faith in me has instilled in me the confidence to pursue my dreams and make a positive impact in the lives of others. Thank you for rooting in me the values of hard work, perseverance, and determination. I am forever grateful for your abiding confidence in me.

To my brothers, who have been my lifelong companions and confidants, thank you for always having my back. Your support and friendship have been invaluable. Our shared experiences have shaped my perspective on life and have contributed to the insights shared within these pages.

I would also like to acknowledge my grandparents, my Nana and Papa, who so completely exemplified the values of integrity and hard work. Your wisdom and guidance have been a guiding light in my life, and I strive to live by the principles you have imparted upon me.

Last, I want to extend my heartfelt appreciation to my team. Your dedication, expertise, and commitment to serving our clients have been the driving force behind our company's growth and success. Without your tireless efforts and support, we would not have been able to manage the remarkable growth we have experienced. Thank you for your hard work and dedication.

To everyone mentioned here, and to those whose names may not be listed but have contributed in their own special way, please accept my deepest gratitude. This book would not have been possible without your support, encouragement, and belief in me. You have all played an integral part in shaping my career and enriching my life, and for that I am truly grateful. May this book serve as a valuable resource to all those seeking a fulfilling retirement.

ABOUT THE AUTHOR

 **Ted Thatcher** is the founder and president of Bright Lake Wealth Management, a financial advisory firm known for its concentration and focus on retirement planning. Ted has dedicated his career to helping individuals and families achieve their retirement goals and secure their financial future.

Ted's journey in the financial industry began in 2012 when he entered the world of private equity investments. With a solid foundation in investment strategies, he quickly recognized the crucial role that comprehensive retirement planning plays in ensuring long-term financial success. Inspired by this realization, Ted transitioned his focus to retirement planning, combining his expertise in investments with his passion for helping others navigate their retirement journey.

With a deep understanding of the unique challenges and complexities of retirement planning, Ted developed the distinguished Launch Your Retirement™ Blueprint, a trademarked planning process that has empowered numerous hardworking individuals and families to navigate their retirement journey with confidence. The Launch Your Retirement™ Planning Process is built upon the five pillars of financial planning: income planning, investment planning, tax planning, healthcare planning, and legacy planning.

In addition to his work at Bright Lake, Ted serves as the chapter president of the American Financial Education Alliance in Redding, California, and Medford, Oregon. In this role, he actively promotes financial literacy and empowers individuals in his community to make informed decisions about their money. Through workshops, educational events, and community outreach programs, Ted is committed to enhancing financial education and fostering a greater understanding of retirement planning among individuals of all backgrounds.

When Ted isn't behind his desk, he enjoys the outdoors with his family, cheering on his Notre Dame Fighting Irish, going on hunting and fishing outings with his father and brothers, and throwing tennis balls across the yard for the family's golden retriever, Finn.

As an author, Ted's passion for educating and empowering individuals shines through in his writing. In this book, *Launch Your Retirement: Your Financial Planning Guide for Going from Saver to Spender*, he distills his years of experience and expertise into a comprehensive resource that demystifies retirement planning and equips readers with the tools they need to create a secure and fulfilling retirement.

His commitment to providing personalized, client-focused solutions has made him a trusted advisor to individuals and families in states across the country.

For more information about Ted Thatcher and his retirement planning expertise, please visit **Launchmyretirement.com** or reach out to **Info@Launchmyretirement.com**.